Celebrating a Canadian heritage...

Those Marvelous Church Suppers

Edited by Elaine Towgood & Anne Nightingale

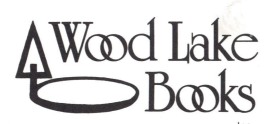
Wood Lake Books Inc.

Text: Ralph Milton
Color Photos: Bob Greichen
Black & White Photos: Ralph Milton
Typesetting: Kari Milton
Proofreading: Norah Kerr

Canadian Cataloguing in Publication Data
Main entry under title:

Those marvelous church suppers

Includes index.
ISBN 0-919599-27-3

1.Cookery. 2.Church entertainments.
I. Nightingale, Anne, 1948-   II. Towgood, Elaine, 1939-
TX715.T496 1985   641.5   C85-091390-X

Copyright©1985 Wood Lake Books, Inc.
All rights reserved. No part of this publication may be reproduced, stored in a retrieval system, or transmitted in any form or by any means, electronic, mechanical, photocopying, recording, or otherwise, without the prior written permission of:

Box 700
Winfield, BC., V0H 2C0

Printed in Canada by
Friesen Printers
Altona, Manitoba,
R0G 0B0

Contents

Cool Drinks and Nibblies — 15
Appetizers, Beverages, Dips & Hors d'oeuvres

Chowders and Soups — 31
Chilled Soups, Seafood Chowders & Hearty Soups

Salads and Veggies — 45
Marinated, Coleslaw, Jellied, Pasta & Make-ahead Salads; Vegetable Casseroles

Main Dishes — 71
Beef, Chicken, Seafood & Pasta Main Dishes; Hamburger Casseroles & 'Mostly' Meatless Dishes

Puddin's and Pies — 111
Cheesecakes, Gelatin Desserts, Pies & Puddings

Cookies, Muffins and more — 137
Yeast Buns, Squares, Cakes, Tarts, Cookies, Muffins & Loaves

Index — 182
A complete list of what's where

*To
the
Marthas*

Foreword

A Celebration of the Marthas

This is really not so much a recipe book as it is a people book; a heritage book; a book of memories and possibilities. It is also a book about what the word "community" means, and about a very special group of people we call the "Marthas".

The first person to suggest that Wood Lake do a cookbook was Glenn Witmer, now head of CBC Enterprises, then one partner in our fledgling Christian publishing ministry. We resisted the idea because, after all, who needs another cookbook.

But ideas are seeds that germinate and sprout and grow into surprising flowers. Eventually the concept of a cookbook blossomed into something far more than a collection of recipes. We began to realize that the church supper, as a Canadian institution, had far more social significance and theological importance than we'd imagined.

As this began to dawn on us, we stopped thinking of this as a *cookbook* (though it is that, and a very good one too!), but rather a book about an experience, a record of something noble and great and fun; something hardly ever recognized for the deep meaning it has in our lives, in our society and in our churches.

To capture some of this meaning, we sent out thousands of letters to church members and church leaders across Canada. We asked them to share their stories, their memories and their recipes.

Our letter seemed to touch a responsive chord in many hearts. It was as if we had pointed out something so obvious, we simply hadn't noticed it. Our letter seemed to trigger an awareness that the Christian community finds one of its deepest expressions in the sharing of a common meal.

As an amateur theologian, I found myself muttering knowingly about the "eucharistic tradition". Ritually, Christian and Jewish communities have shared that meaning in the celebration of the Jewish Passover, or the Christian Mass, Eucharist, Communion, and Lord's Supper. The ritual feast goes by many names and it has many nuances of theology and tradition. The "communal meal" emphasis is probably strongest in Protestant Christianity. But in every tradition, the ritual meal symbolizes (among other things) the community of faith.

While the eucharistic meal is the subject of much discussion by church scholars, the church supper tradition is seldom examined. It is hardly ever the subject of theological discourse, and not often seen as an important ritual of the church. That's probably as it should be.

The church supper belongs to the lay people. For them, it has a meaning (seldom articulated) that is deep and real and powerful. It recalls a coming together out of the wilderness of prairie and bush and ocean, out of the desert of loneliness into the promised land of community and fellowship.

The potluck supper was born out of loneliness and poverty. It celebrates the wealth of faith and community; of sharing the little that we have and the little that we are.

That act of sharing became a ritual of community. That act of sitting down at a table brought people together in an act of bonding that no speech or ceremony could have accomplished. It is a truly ecumenical ritual, in that people in almost every society around the world use food as a symbol of unity.

For ordinary people, who have read neither anthroplogy or theology, the whole thing is just a matter of "being friendly". But I suspect it may be for many a higher "communion" than the more formal eucharist.

Bishop Remi De Roo of Victoria writes: "The more remote the setting, as in tiny mission outposts on the West Coast, the more church suppers impress me as something vitally human. People come together to experience the warmth of ever-renewed friendships, the reality of mutual interdependence, the love of sisters and brothers in Christ. Sharing the food we bring to others, we come to know that we are one in Jesus our Lord."

Church suppers have been an inclusive ritual. They were among the first ventures in ecumenical Christianity in Canada.

Sr. Katherine McCaffrey of the Canadian Religious Conference says that "as a child, long before the ecumenical movement, my most pleasant the positive memories of Christians of other faiths came from attending their church suppers."

The church supper was inclusive in other ways. So many of the stories told in this book reflect the fact that children, left out of so many church functions, were welcome at the church supper. In fact it's children that help make those church suppers "marvelous".

In earlier times, when food was sometimes scarce, children were often ecouraged to eat far more heartily than normally allowed or possible at home. "Once a year, we could eat all the chicken we wanted, and we felt like kings." Perhaps that is true now as well, with children of the "hidden poor".

Foreword

This book symbolizes the essential oneness of the church supper, where the Bishop gets into a conversation with a child and the Moderator pours coffee for its mother.

We must be careful, of course, not to let sentimentality get the best of us. Church suppers are sometimes rigid, exclusive affairs, that are destructive of community. And sometimes they become competitive displays of wealth that are an offense to anyone with a sense of world justice. Every human institution is subject to abuse, and the church supper is no exception.

This book is not an analysis of the church supper. It is simply a celebration.

It tries to reflect some of what is good; to celebrate the spirit of inclusive community. There are recipes here from the Prime Minister, a Bishop, a current Moderator and several past Moderators, famous authors, editors, clergy, church members of many denominations, and children. They are side by side, with no distinction made between them. And as the editors discovered very early in the extensive testing of these recipes, "the best recipes do *not necessarily* come from people who are famous."

Lastly, but certainly not least, this book is "the revenge of the Marthas." That's how church historian Bob Stewart of Vancouver described this book. I'd prefer to call it a "celebration of the Marthas."

Bob was talking about the people, most of them women, who are out there in the kitchen doing the *necessary* things. They are the "keepers of the hearth", the ones who seldom get the glory, but without whom the world would come to a whimpering halt. They are the Marthas, named after the woman in the story told by Luke (10; 38-42).

"The reality of putting on such a feast," Bob points out, "was not so much fun as the memory of it some years later. The memory of hot stoves and dirty dishes fades more quickly than the memory of warm fellowship and heaping platters. This is likely as it should be, though I can hardly believe that the 'Marthas' did not occasionally contemplate a slave revolt."

They did more than contemplate. Not a few women's groups in churches of all denominations dug in their heels and refused to cater for yet another dinner. A few complimentary words from the minister and the dirty dishes to wash, was simply not enough reward for all that work.

People like Nellie McClung led the battle to get women out of the kitchens and into the pulpits. I'm not aware that she said it, but it most certainly crossed her mind that it would be good for all if the people in the pulpits got into the kitchens from time to time.

Nowadays, it is becoming more usual to see men pitching in with the women in doing the hard work associated with church suppers. Nevertheless, it is still the women who do most of the thinking, planning and work. There are notable exceptions, and it is gratifying that many of the recipes in this book come from men. But they *are* the exceptions.

I don't suppose there are any statistics anywhere that would reflect the dollars, probably millions of dollars, raised through the hard work of putting on church suppers. Nor is there any record of how many congregations would have collapsed, had it not been for the faithful work of the Marthas (both male and female) who peeled potatoes until their fingers literally bled.

Of course, it wasn't just the money the Marthas raised, though that was phenomenal. Those church suppers were the cement that held the church community together, that enabled the clergy to say from the pulpit on Sunday, "We are one in the Lord!" and for the people to reply, "We are one indeed!"

It has often been said that God calls us, not to success, but to faithfulness. That's one of those statements which the church often affirms but seldom lives. There are bronze plaques in the churches for those who died for their faith, but few plaques to honor those, who day by day by day, lived for their faith. The heroes we hold up to our young people are those who climb mountains, fight battles, win victories and make speeches. Perhaps, if we were able to practise what we profess, we might look for our heroes in the kitchens.

The real monument to the Marthas is the continuing church itself. The buildings, yes, but its life too. Our church owes its life to the millions of Marthas, far more than to the orators, scholars and administrators.

As a tribute to the Marthas, this book is too little, too late. But it is dedicated with both apologies and thanks to the Marthas.

May God forgive us for taking you for granted!

Ralph Milton
Publisher

To all those who helped Thanks!

Many, many people helped with this book. Hundreds offered encouragement and support; others offered recipes, memories, poems and stories. Some smiled when we took their photos. Others have decided to help sell this cookbook to raise money for their congregations, for world mission, and for the ministry of Wood Lake Books.

To all of you, our sincerest thanks. We've tried to make a list below of some of the people who have helped. But the list is incomplete.

So thanks to the many people listed below who helped or contributed in one way or another. And a very *special* thanks to those who offered their support, but whose names do not appear below.

Florence Anderson, Creston, B.C.
Irene Anderson, Keremeos, B.C.
Muriel Arnold, Sicamous, B.C.
Bev Ashbaugh, Vernon, B.C.
Martha Ashbaugh, Kamloops, B.C.
Hazel Backus, Vancouver, B.C.
Dan Bailey, Wolfville, N.S.
Doreen Bain, Kelowna, B.C.
Revs. Glen & Pat Baker, Kelowna, B.C.
Rita Baker, Petrolia, Ont.
Hazel Baldwin, Westbank, B.C.
Bernice Balfour, Vancouver, B.C.
Bruce Balfour, Vancouver, B.C.
Ruth Baren, Yellow Grass, Sask.
M.L. Barmby, Yellow Grass, Sask.
Rev. Phyllis Barnes, St. Mary's, Ont.
Eva Bartee, Westbank, B.C.
Shirley Bathgate, Kelowna, B.C.
Penny Battle, Don Mills, Ont.
Marj Bell, Winfield, B.C.
Ruth Bell, Deloraine, Man.
Elna Biccum, Kelowna, B.C.
Connie Bickford, Burnaby, B.C.
Donna Blois, Vernon, B.C.
Rev. Rod & Maria Booth, Willowdale, Ont.
Bonnie Brennan, Ottawa, Ont.
Darryll Brock, Estevan, Sask.
Wolly Brons, Enderby, B.C.
Ethel Buck, Vancouver, B.C.
Susan Butler-Jones, Sault Ste. Marie, Ont.
Helen Butling, Nelson, B.C.
Dot Cann, Kelowna, B.C.
Genevieve Carder, Scarborough, Ont.
M.W. Chepesuik, Kelowna, B.C.
Glenna Christophers, Winfield, B.C.
Rev. Gail C. Christy, Yellow Grass, Sask.
Rev. Gordon & June Churchill, Rockyford, Alta.
Betty Lou Clark, Edmonton, Alta.
Phil & Audrey Cline, Toronto, Ont.
Anna M. Coles, Vancouver, B.C.
Iris Cornelson, Westbank, B.C.
Jean Cowling, Westbank, B.C.
Catherine Craig, Abbotsford, B.C.
Agnes Cunningham, Kelowna, B.C.
Anne Cunningham, Calgary, Alta.
Beryl Dalgliesh, Kelowna, B.C.
Jean Daniels, Winfield, B.C.
Jean Davidson, Sicamous, B.C.
William Davis, Toronto, Ont.
Paul De Groot, Edmonton, Alta.
Most Rev. Remi De Roo, Victoria, B.C.
Betty DeBeck, Kamloops, B.C.
Gwen Dewhurst, Westbank, B.C.
Enid Dorward, Winnipeg, Man.
Melody Drewlo, Winfield, B.C.
Cheryll Doull, Souris, Man.
Olive Dove, Kamloops, B.C.
Muriel Duncan, Toronto, Ont.
Mr. & Mrs. Sherman Embree, Sr., Vancouver
Mrs. Howell Evans, Hudson, Que.
Ivy Fallow, Winfield, B.C.
Rev. Walter & Joan Farquharson, Saltcoats, Sask.
Esther Faubert, Sicamous, B.C.
Barbara Ferris, Kelowna, B.C.
Toni Fibick, Westbank, B.C.
Betty Fines, Orangeville, Ont.
Gwen Finlayson, Kelowna, B.C.
Doug Flanders, Toronto, Ont.
Carol Fletcher, Winfield, B.C.
Diane Forrest, Toronto, Ont.
Gertrude Fox, Westbank, B.C.
Coira Freeman, Victoria, B.C.
Dianne Friesen, Winfield, B.C.
Jim Frogley, Happy Valley, Labrador
Elizabeth Funge, Collingwood, N.S.
Mabel Gamble, Mannville, Alta.

Marjorie George, Corner Brook, Nfld.
Marjorie Glaicar, Armstrong, B.C.
Janie Goodwin, Kelowna, B.C.
Lily Granigan, Wainwright, Alta.
Margaret Grant, Vancouver, B.C.
Sheila Gear, Vancouver, B.C.
Bonnie Green, Toronto, Ont.
Anita Greenaway, West Vancouver, B.C.
Rev. Betty Griffiths-Ling, Shediac, N.B.
Irene Hallisey, Kelowna, B.C.
Marj Hannah, Kelowna, B.C.
Dr. Bob Hatfield, Calgary, Alta.
Laura Hawthorn, Bracebridge, Ont.
Rev. G.R. & Linda Haynes, Vancouver, B.C.
Mary Henderson, Calgary, Alta.
Peggy Henderson, Lucknow, Ont.
Katie Hignell, Vancouver, B.C.
Justice & Mrs. George Hill, Estevan, Sask.
Dr. Gerald Hobbs, Vancouver, B.C.
Lois Hole, Kelowna, B.C.
Karen & Dave Holmes, Vancouver, B.C.
Diane Hoornaert, Winfield, B.C.
Florence Howard, New Westminster, B.C.
Verna Howarth, Winnipeg, Man.
Berna Hull, Don Mills, Ont.
Evelyn Hunt, Westbank, B.C.
Rev. Bob Hunter, Calgary, Alta.
Judy Hutchinson, Edmonton, Alta.
Madeline Ingledew, Victoria, B.C.
Rev. Brian Jackson, Vernon, B.C.
Pat Johnson, Kamloops, B.C.
Muriel Jones, Edmonton, Alta.
Miss Chimaki Kamakura, Tokyo, Japan
Jack Kampf, Abbotsford, B.C.
Grace Kanwisher, Ottawa, Ont.
Margaret Kawano, Winfield, B.C.
Howard & Eileen Kent, Westbank, B.C.
Frances Klein, Kelowna, B.C.
Barbara Klich, Downsview, Ont.
Mary Klochko, Kamsack, Sask.
Ron & Kris Klusmeier, Cascade, Wis.
Grace Knott, Wainwright, Alta.
David Kuhn, Wolfville, N.S.
Orma K. Kyle, Vancouver, B.C.
Marie Ladd, Westbank, B.C.
Anne Land, Okanagan Centre, B.C.
Langley United Ladies Group, Langley, B.C.
Margaret Laurence, Lakefield, Ont.
Ida Lauridsen, Rockyford, Alta.
Margaret Lawson, Don Mills, Ont.
Fr. John M. Lee, Lloydminster, Alta.
Audrey Leonard, Winfield, B.C.
Ellen Link, Kelowna, B.C.
Pat Litke, Calgary, Alta.

Paula Locke, Vancouver, B.C.
Margaret & Douglas MacArthur, Trail, B.C.
Mimi MacIntyre, Hamilton, Ont.
Viola Manery, Keremeos, B.C.
Mrs. Lee Maranchuk, Kelowna, B.C.
Jessie Mawhinney, Kelowna, B.C.
Pegeen McAskill, Vancouver, B.C.
Sr. Katherine McCaffrey, Ottawa, Ont.
Phyllis McCallum, Saltcoats, Sask.
Pat McCoubrey, Winfield, B.C.
Dr. Hugh McCullum, Toronto, Ont.
Julie Mezaros, Penticton, B.C.
Gwendolyn Mills, Meadow Lake, Sask.
Mrs. M. Mills, Georgetown, Ont.
Rev. Bev Milton, Winfield, B.C.
Rev. W.P. Mittler, Marmora, Ont.
Rev. Mary Morgan, Dundas, Ont.
Georgina Morine, Wolfville, N.S.
Anne Mueller, Sicamous, B.C.
Brian Mulroney, Ottawa, Ont.
Garth Mundle, Edmonton, Alta.
Lorraine Munro, Winfield, B.C.
Rev. Walter Murray, Wolfville, N.S.
Tom Neal, Saltcoats, Sask.
Anne Nightingale, Okanagan Centre, B.C.
Willa Nowell, Westbank, B.C.
Margaret Osborne, Kelowna, B.C.
Palermo U.C.W., Oakville, Ont.
Florence Parkinson, Kelowna, B.C.
Edith Parkyn, Vernon, B.C.
Rev. Gary Paterson, Vancouver, B.C.
Ilene Patterson, Winfield, B.C.
Donna Peaker, Vernon, B.C.
Gladys Perkins, Kelowna, B.C.
Myrna Phillips, Ellerslie, P.E.I.
Laura Phillips, Arlington, P.E.I.
Jean Pierce, Ouispamsis, N.B.
Joan Prentice, Vancouver, B.C.
Linda Price, Calgary, Alta.
Linda Prouten, Langley, B.C.
Margaret Pursley, Palermo, Ont.
Mrs. Hayward Pye, Corner Brook, Nfld.
Mary Quarry, Kelowna, B.C.
Joy B. Quigley, Kelowna, B.C.
Ed Read, Westbank, B.C.
Gertrude Rella, Rossland, B.C.
Alan Reynolds, Vancouver, B.C.
Rev. Celia Ricker, Regina, Sask.
Cathy Roxburgh,
Mrs. G. Sakatch,
Deborah Ann Sanford, Petawawa, Ont.
Rev. Allan & Megumi Saunders, Estevan, Sask.
Margaret Schneider, Meadow Lake, Sask.
Dorothy Scott, Westbank, B.C.

Thanks! — 11

Athelene Secret, Kelowna, B.C.
Sue Sewell, Kamloops, B.C.
Rev. John & Helen Shearman, Oakville, Ont.
Chris Shennon, Winfield, B.C.
Donna Sinclair, North Bay, Ont.
Dr. Ted Siverns, Kelowna, B.C.
Rt. Rev. Robert F. Smith, Vancouver, B.C.
Mrs. S.J. Smith, Victoria, B.C.
Marj & Wallace Smith, Ellerslie, P.E.I.
Dorothy Snodgrass, Westbank, B.C.
Connie Spooner, Edmonton, Alta.
Anne M. Squire, Toronto, Ont.
St. John's Ecumenical Parish, Keremeos, B.C.
Karen & Neale Stead, Winfield, B.C.
Rev. William Steadman, Forest, Ont.
Rhoda Stein, Burnaby, B.C.
Bob Stewart, Vancouver, B.C.
Sheila Storry, Wolfville, N.S.
Jean Swann, Westbank, B.C.
Irene Szakal, Kelowna, B.C.
Bill Taylor, Vancouver, B.C.
Kay Taylor, Winfield, B.C.
Heather Tyler, Winfield, B.C.
Mardi Tindal, Campbellville, Ont.
Mrs. Bert Topham, Grandview, Man.
Elaine Towgood, Oyama, B.C.
Bev Turner, Kelowna, B.C.
Rev. G.E. Waddell, Newdale, Man.
Elly Walraven, Kelowna, B.C.
Thomas J. Walton, Burlington, Ont.
Fiona and Ron Warrington, Fort McMurray, Alta.
Alice Weidman, Westbank, B.C.
West Point Grey Presbyterian Church, Vancouver
Margaret Young, Vancouver, B.C.

The cooking class at the George Elliot High School in Winfield, B.C. deserves a word of thanks; especially their teacher, Susan Bowman.

While most of the recipes were tested in Elaine Towgood and Anne Nightingale's own kitchens, they felt it would be useful if some of the recipes might be tested by less experienced cooks. So they talked to Miss Bowman, who was more than happy to help.

"What a great bunch of people!" was Elaine's comment after she and Anne had spent several sessions with the class. "They worked hard, and they were fun." Elaine and Anne had special praise for Miss Bowman whom they liked as a person and admired as a teacher. The students participating in the program were:

Tillie Andrews
June Baran
Dan Cawston
Melodie Chilton
Sherry Dean
Kathy Gallacher

Maria Gysen
Kevin Harder
Anne Kandola
Michele Murray
Kelly Niles

Mike Patterson
Debbie Solberg
Mandy Vreeswijk
Dana Wentworth
Jim Widing

*All the royalties
from the sale of this book
are being donated
to Canada's churches,
to help them with their work
in the Third World.*

A grace...

*God of power
our creator, sustainer and redeemer,
you have called us
to make of our lives a celebration;
a communion
we share with all creation.
We thank you for this feast;
this food which strengthens us,
this fellowship which warms us,
and this faith
which empowers us.
Amen.*

This concentrate is handy to keep in the refrigerator for instant summer thirst quenchers. It can be used in any recipe in place of frozen concentrated lemonade. It was sent to us by Ethel Buck, who is a member of Ryerson United Church in Vancouver.

Ethel Buck's Lemonade Syrup

6	**lemons,** juice & rind	6
9 cups	**sugar**	2.25 L
2 Tbsp	**citric acid**	30 mL
1 Tbsp	**tartaric acid**	15 mL
6 cups	**boiling water**	1.5 L

Makes about 10 cups (2.5 L).

Grate lemons; squeeze the juice. Combine sugar, acids, juice & rind in a large bowl. Add boiling water & stir until sugar is dissolved.

Cool. Strain if desired. Store in covered jars in refrigerator—will keep for months.

To serve, mix approximately 1 part syrup to 6 parts water & pour over ice.

Rhubarb grows well in Calgary's foothills climate. For that matter it grows well almost anywhere in Canada and is the first fresh fruit to be ready in the spring.

This drink is a hit, even with people who don't really care for rhubarb. It was sent to us by Linda Price of the Campbell-Stone church in Calgary; an exciting congregation where the Disciples-Church of Christ and the United Church worship together.

Linda Price's Rhubarb Punch

16 cups	**rhubarb**	4 L
3 qts	**water**	3 L
3 cups	**sugar**	750 mL
¾ cup	**lemon juice**	180 mL
12½ oz	**orange juice**, frozen concentrate	355 mL
4-26 oz	**gingerale**, bottles	4-750 mL

Makes about 8 qts (8 L).

Wash fresh rhubarb & cut into 2" (5 cm) pieces. Combine in *large* cooking pot with water, bring to a boil & simmer till tender. Strain the juice into another pot & add sugar to hot juice, stirring till dissolved. Chill. (Juice could be frozen at this point for future use.)

When ready to use, add lemon juice, frozen orange juice concentrate & chilled gingerale, along with lots of ice cubes.

Like the sugar in our tea...

Here's a delightful "grace" from an old Newfoundland layreader named William Newbury. It was sent to us by Jim Frogley of Happy Valley, Labrador.

> "Lord, bless the food
>   upon these dishes,
> As thou didst bless
>   the loaves and fishes.
> And like the sugar
>   in our tea,
> May our spirits, O Lord,
>   be stirred by Thee!"

Cool Drinks and Nibbles

We encountered a delightful strawberry punch at a clergy gathering in Kelowna one hot spring day. It was prepared by Rev. Patricia Baker of First United in Kelowna.

This recipe is very similar, and is a delight served in tall glasses with lots of ice cubes. Pat left a bunch of whole strawberries floating on top of the punch bowl, which was a nice tasty touch.

Pat Baker's Strawberry Punch

1½ cups	**strawberries**, crushed	375 mL
½ cup	**sugar**	125 mL
2 cups	**cold tea**	500 mL
2-12½ oz	**pink lemonade**, frozen concentrate	2-355 mL
26 oz	**gingerale**, bottle	750 mL
26 oz	**club soda**, bottle	750 mL

Makes about 12 cups (3 L).

In blender or food processor, puree *fresh* or *frozen* strawberries with sugar & tea.

Just before serving, mix together strawberry puree, lemonade concentrate, gingerale & club soda in large punch bowl or pitcher.

Serve in tall glasses with lots of ice cubes.

Photo: Berkeley Studio

This is a tasty and a fun drink sent to us by Paul De Groot, the Religion Editor for the Edmonton Journal. Paul is an active member of the Christian Reformed Church and works hard to support the Institute for Christian Studies in Toronto.

"This recipe is not original," says Paul, "but then journalists rarely are. But it will keep alive the myth that while journalists can't cook, they do know how to drink."

BOP is great to serve to gatherings of church people, especially when they come from various denominations. Be sure to read them Paul's "exegesis" of BOP. It's hilarious!

Paul De Groot's BOP

1	**banana**	1
1 cup	**orange juice**	250 mL
1 cup	**pineapple juice**	250 mL

Combine ingredients in blender & blend until smooth.

Variations are endless! Ten year-old Cathy didn't care for BOP until strawberries were added turning it pink, her favorite color! (which, of course, also turned BOP into BOPS). Add an egg or milk & VOILA!— instant breakfast!

The Theology of BOP

Like many significant religious questions, the exegesis of BOP is deceptively simple. The letters are simply an acronym for its prime ingredients, banana, orange and pineapple juice. Nevertheless, with minimal effort, the process can be made sufficiently obscure and difficult to interest almost any seasoned theologian.

I have been operating on the hypothesis that BOP was very popular among the Corinthians in the years of the early church, and its variations have become part of various church traditions.

For the moment, however, let us be content with the knowledge that this drink is capable of covering more ground, ecclesiastically, than any other recipe I know. It is suitable for any occasion, from a fundamentalist prayer breakfast to a liberal, mainline New Year's Eve party.

This recipe has several levels of development, but we'll begin at its most simplistic— fundamentalist BOP. It is a simple trinity of three juices. Since that adds up to less than three cups of juice, you'll want to add something truly American, like a bit of Coke for "life".

Baptists and Calvinists will want to add a couple of ice cubes. Baptists for the water, and Calvinists for the chill. As a Calvinist, I know that there's nothing like a dose of Calvinism to cool off an otherwise warm occasion.

Members of the Eastern Orthodox church should add a raw egg, in keeping with their emphasis on Easter. It adds richness and body.

Roman Catholics should add very little, but in keeping with their tradition of using small amounts of liquid (e.g. chrism, a sip of wine at mass, baptism by sprinkling, etc.) in various rites, we can make BOP sacramental by adding a few drops of vanilla. Anglicans can achieve the same result with just a dash of sherry.

People in the United Church make BOP their own by adding a small glass of Welch's grape juice and floating a small square of white bread on top. It does turn the drink rather grey and the bread mushy, but that should not be considered representative of United Church theology.

For those who are big believers in the gospel of prosperity (I am not brave enough to give them a name; but don't let that stop you), a bit of sugar will mask the tart, earthy flavor of this drink and make it appropriately sweet.

The liberal mainliner who is never satisfied with ordinary theology will no doubt add a dash of vodka to help dull the sharp edges of reality. It also helps them keep their composure when arguing with fundamentalists.

BOP, in all its variations, is heavenly. You will decide for yourself whether that is a theological or culinary assessment.

Paul De Groot

Mary Morgan is a "Spiritual Director-Minister" at the Woodlands Center for Renewal in Dundas, Ontario. Denominationally, she calls herself a Baptist-Quaker but she says, "I don't know if that makes me a Quakerist or a Baker!"

Mary found some raspberries and mint growing side by side. That struck her as interesting, and so she invented Raspberry Mintel. The drink was served at a garden dinner which her community celebrated with neighbors.

For that occasion, Mary wrote one of the few prayers that would be appropriate to say with a drink in your hand.

"Lord, I thank you that the raspberries and mint were growing side by side. May I ever be reminded of your bountiful giving, and that eating can be a time of connection with others, because we too are growing side by side. May this meal draw us closer together. Amen."

Mary Morgan's
Raspberry Mintel

2 Tbsp	**sugar**	60 mL
½ cup	**mint leaves**, fresh	125 mL
1 cup	**boiling water**	250 mL
1½ cups	**raspberries**, fresh or frozen	375 mL
6 oz	**orange juice**, frozen concentrate	170 mL
2 cups	**cold water**	500 mL

Makes 8 servings.

Combine sugar, mint leaves and 1 cup (250 mL) boiling water. Let this stand for 5 minutes. Remove mint leaves.

Mash raspberries. Combine with mint syrup & orange concentrate & stir until well blended. Add 2 cups (500 mL) cold water. Strain if desired. Serve over ice with fresh mint leaves.

Raspberries may be frozen & put in the freezer, & a pot of mint can be brought in from the garden in the fall so that this drink may be enjoyed year round. The red/green colors make it especially nice at Christmas time.

A Newfoundland toast:

First person: "Raisin' me glass, I look t'ards ye."
Second person: "Catchin' yer eye I nods accordin'."

Calypso Punch has a subtle, cinnamon flavor combined with the fruit juices. It comes from Myrna Phillips of Ellerslie, P.E.I. It's a delightful change of pace.

Myrna Phillips' Calypso Punch

3	cinnamon sticks	3
¼ cup	sugar	60 mL
2 cups	water	500 mL
2 cups	pineapple juice	500 mL
1 cup	orange juice	250 mL
¼ cup	lemon juice	60 mL
26 oz	gingerale	750 mL
2 trays	ice cubes	2 trays

Makes approx. 2 qts (2 L).

Simmer cinnamon sticks & sugar in water for 10 minutes. Cool & remove cinnamon sticks (they can be re-used).

Chill ingredients. Combine fruit juices & sugar syrup in chilled punch bowl. Slowly pour in ginger ale.

Instead of plain ice cubes, freeze some of the fruit juice so punch will not be diluted.

Garnish punch bowl with lemon and orange slices & mint leaves.

After five services, he was bushed...

Few people remember church suppers better than young ministers out in their first parish. Their young appetites and the care-giving instincts of country families often resulted in the young clergy eating rather well. Besides, it was an honor to have the minister over for a meal.

Rev. Rod Booth, who is now with the Division of Communication of the United Church in Toronto, remembers those meals, and one marvelous mix-up.

It had been a long, strenuous day. He'd preached at five services and he was bushed. That's why he was glad for an on-the-spot invitation from Dot Weston for a meal.

"I was just finishing a large slice of Dot's marvelous apple pie when the phone rang. It was the Betts, wondering where their minister was.

"Flustered, tired, and feeling very full, I arrived to find an enormous roast beef dinner waiting for me. To make matters worse, they had already gone ahead and eaten, and now the whole family was gathered at the table to watch the minister enjoy his meal.

"But they'd saved one important function for me. I was to ask the blessing. All heads were dutifully bowed around the table.

"By now thoroughly undone, to my horror I heard my own voice begin with the familiar words: 'Now I lay me down to sleep...'!"

These two drinks have lots of spirit but of the right kind. They come from Thomas Walton who works for the Abstainers' Insurance Company in Burlington, Ontario.

The Jungle Juice is a refreshing pick-me-up that could almost be a substitute for breakfast. The Coffee Fantasia is definitely not for the calorie conscious, but will be especially enjoyed by coffee lovers.

Thomas Walton's Jungle Juice

1 cup	**pineapple juice**	250 mL	
2	**bananas**	2	
1 cup	**plain yogurt**	250 mL	
2	**pineapple** wedges	2	

Makes 2 tall drinks.

In a blender, mix the juice, banana & yogurt. Pour into glasses, garnish with pineapple wedges.

Coffee Fantasia

1 cup	**cold coffee**	250 mL
2 scoops	**ice cream**, chocolate	2 scoops
¼ cup	**whipping cream**	60 mL
2 Tbsp	**rum extract**	30 mL
2 tsp	**almond extract**	10 mL

Makes 2 tall drinks.

Blend or shake & pour over crushed ice.

Cheese lovers will enjoy these contributions from Hazel Backus of Vancouver and Anne Land of Okanagan Centre, B.C. These crispy mouthfuls are a welcome addition to an appetizer tray, to serve at a Bible study group, or with fruit in children's lunches.

Hazel Backus' Cheese Crisps

½ cup	**butter**, softened	125 mL
½ lb	**cheddar cheese**, grated	225 g
1 cup	**flour**	250 mL
1½ cups	**rice crisps cereal**	375 mL

Makes 3 dozen

Preheat oven to 350ºF.

Combine softened butter & grated cheese with wooden spoon until creamy. Add flour & mix thoroughly. Lastly, work in cereal.

With hands, form into flattened balls & place on greased cookie sheet.

Bake at 350ºF. for about 10 minutes, or until lightly browned.

Anne Land's Cheese Straws

1 cup	**flour**	250 mL
¼ tsp	**baking powder**	1 mL
½ tsp	**salt**	2 mL
dash	**cayenne**	dash
½ cup	**butter**	125 mL
1 cup	**cheddar cheese**, grated	250 mL

Makes about 3 dozen.

Preheat oven to 350ºF.

Sift together flour, baking powder, salt & cayenne. Cut butter in with pastry blender till crumbly. Lastly, stir in grated cheese. Form mixture into a ball & knead gently till smooth.

Roll out to 1/8" (.3 cm) thickness & cut into desired shape *or* form into a roll as for ice box cookies; cut into slices. Place on cookie sheet.

Bake at 350ºF. for 15 minutes.

In our prepublication testing, this antipasto rated top marks every time. One gentleman said "This gets 10 out of 10. And I'm Italian."

It comes from Fiona Warrington of Fort McMurray. A very similar recipe came from Donna Peaker of Vernon, who sent us such a delightful story about "Operation Talent" that we decided to name it after Trinity United, where she is the secretary.

Unlike many antipastos, this one is very easy to make because it uses mostly canned veggies. What's more, you can watch out for sales of canned veggies throughout the year, so the pre-Christmas antipasto project won't be such a shock to your budget.

Fiona Warrington's Trinity Antipasto

60 oz	ketchup	1.7 L
¾ cup	vinegar	180 mL
½ cup	olive oil	125 mL
4 tsp	coarse salt	20 mL
1	cauliflower	1
1	green pepper	1
2-10 oz	green beans, can	2-284 mL
10 oz	mushrooms, can	284 mL
1 qt	dill pickles	1 L
8 oz	pickled onions, jar	250 g
4 oz	green olives, jar	113 g
4½ oz	ripe olives, can chopped	128 mL
2-6½ oz	solid tuna, can	2-184 g
2-3½ oz	shrimp, can	2-113 g

Makes 14 pts (7 L).

Boil ketchup, vinegar, olive oil & salt for 10 minutes in large cooking pot. Remove from heat.

Blanch cauliflower in boiling water for 2 minutes. Drain, rinse & break into flowerets & chop medium fine. Wash & chop green pepper. Drain & discard liquid from beans, mushrooms, dill pickles, pickled onions, green olives & ripe olives. Chop. Drain tuna & break into pieces. Drain & rinse shrimp. Add all of the above to ketchup sauce. Stir well & let stand 15 minutes.

Spoon into sterilized pint jars, seal & process 15 minutes.

Mend a broken heart...

Every meal should be begun with a word of thanks to God. Dr. Garth Mundle, Principal of St. Stephen's College in Edmonton, shares a beautiful thought on prayer which he found in the *New Hebrew Prayer Book* .

"Prayer invites God's presence to nourish our spirits and God's will to prevail in our lives. Prayer cannot bring water to parched fields, nor mend a broken bridge, nor rebuild a ruined city, but prayer can water an arid soul, mend a broken heart, and rebuild a weakened will."

Operation Talent

"Operation Talent started so innocently, it seemed" says Donna Peaker of Vernon, B.C. "All I did was what I do every day. I took the mail in to Brian Jackson, one of the ministers at our church.

"He took out his wallet and handed me a $50.00 bill. Just like that. Then he told me to go home and read Matthew 25: 14-31 and report back to the Congregation in 10 days time.

"My heart sank. I already knew what the Bible passage said. It was the story Jesus told about the rich person who gave ten talents to one of the servants, five talents to another, and one talent to a third.

"I phoned my husband for sympathy. I was far too busy for anything like this. Then I read on to the 31st verse and I knew I had to go into this one hundred percent.

"What should I do? Buy a sweepstake ticket? Run away? How far would fifty dollars get me?

"That's when Donna Blois came into the office, and simply sank into a chair. 'Has Brian been giving you money too?' I asked. She nodded wearily.

"There was nothing to do but to do something. We decided to pool our resources. 'Maybe we should buy Brian a one-way bus ticket somewhere,' I said. Finally we decided to make antipasto to sell after church that Sunday. We didn't have much time or money, but we felt sure we had enough friends at Trinity who would help us out by buying antipasto. We made 60 jars of the stuff.

"We were sold out in ten minutes and taking orders for more! So we went into production again. Have you any idea how many onions we peeled or olives we diced?

"But we sold out again. And we reported to the congregation that we had made $400; enough to return Brian's seed money and to give $150 to our denomination's mission fund and $150 to the Salvation Army Food Bank.

"Definitely a success story. From almost every angle. But now, when I see Brian reach for his wallet, I run!"

Dianne Friesen of Winfield, B.C. does a number of things very well. One of them is conducting the kids' choir at the Winfield United Church.

Another is to make this Crab Mousse, which is a rich, molded appetizer that looks attractive on a tray surrounded by a variety of crackers. But it's not something she serves to her kids' choir.

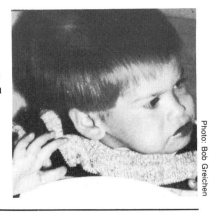

Photo: Bob Greichen

Dianne Friesen's Crab Mousse

10 oz	**mushroom soup**, can	284 mL
6 oz	**cream cheese**	170 g
1 env.	**unflavored gelatin**	1 env.
¼ cup	**cold water**	60 mL
½ cup	**celery**, finely chopped	125 mL
½ cup	**green onion**, finely chopped	125 mL
1 cup	**mayonnaise**	250 mL
1-4 oz	**crabmeat**, tin rinsed & broken up	113 g
¼ tsp	**curry powder** (optional)	1 mL

Makes 20 appetizer servings.

In a small saucepan, heat soup & cream cheese, stirring till smooth.

Sprinkle gelatin over cold water in small dish & let stand 5 minutes. Add gelatin mixture to soup. Add celery, green onion, mayonnaise, crabmeat & curry powder. Mix well.

Pour into a lightly greased 4 cup (1 L) mold & allow to chill overnight in fridge.

Memories of Marriage Encounter...

Here's a grace sent to us by Janie Goodwin of St. David's Presbyterian Church in Kelowna. It is sung to the tune of Edelweiss, and will bring many powerful memories to those people who have been to a Marriage Encounter weekend.

"Bless this house, bless this food,
Come, dear Lord, and sit with us.
May our talk glow with love,
Come with your love to surround us.
Friendship and love
May they bloom and grow.
Bloom and grow forever.
Bless our friends. Bless our food.
Bless all people together."

Fiona Warrington of Fort McMurray is well known as a very fine cook. Her shrimp dip is delicious with assorted vegetables, chips or crackers. Other seafood such as salmon, tuna or crab can be substituted for the shrimp. If you're using this as a chip-dip, you may want to thin it with added sour cream.

This dip may account for the fact that whenever the Marriage Encounter Spiral had a meeting, they always wanted to go to Fiona and Ron's.

Fiona Warrington's Shrimp Dip

8 oz	**cream cheese**, pkg	225 mL
¼ cup	**mayonnaise**	60 mL
2 tsp	**lemon juice**	10 mL
2 Tbsp	**onion**, grated	30 mL
5 oz	**shrimp**, can	150 g
¼ tsp	**Worcestershire sauce**	1 mL
	salt & **pepper**, to taste	

Makes 1½ cups (375 mL).

Combine softened cream cheese with mayonnaise & lemon juice; mix until smooth. Add onion & drained shrimp to mixture & stir gently. Lastly add worcestershire sauce & salt & pepper to taste.

Cover & store in fridge if not using right away.

Rev. Gary Paterson is on the staff of the B.C. Conference of the United Church. That job has him trotting all over the province, and keeps him more than busy. Maybe that's why he enjoys this recipe for Eggplant Dip. It's an easy blender recipe that is excellent with a variety of raw vegies.

Gary Paterson's Eggplant Dip

1	eggplant	1	
1 or 2	garlic cloves	1 or 2	
1 tsp	oregano	5 mL	
2 Tbsp	red wine vinegar	30 mL	
⅓ cup	olive oil	85 mL	
3 Tbsp	parsley	45 mL	
3 Tbsp	green onions	45 mL	
1/8 tsp	hot pepper sauce	.5 mL	
¼ tsp	salt	1 mL	

Makes about 2 cups (500 mL).

Preheat oven to 350°F.

Bake eggplant in preheated oven for approximately 1 hour, or until very soft. Scoop out flesh, discarding skin & stem.

Spoon eggplant pulp into blender container. Mince garlic clove & add to eggplant: add oregano, vinegar & olive oil. Finely chop the parsley & green onions. Add to above along with hot pepper sauce & salt. Blend till smooth. Chill.

Can food be blessed retroactively?

Dr. Robert Smith, Moderator of the United Church of Canada, has been called upon to say many prayers for many occasions. On one occasion, he was asked to say grace at a potluck supper where many of the people had already begun to eat. Can food be blessed retroactively?

Apparently it can, and with the use of Psalm 103. So Dr. Smith prayed, "Bless the Lord, O my soul, and all that is within me, bless God's holy name."

A delightful way to share...

Please send _____ copies (at 12^{95}, plus $1 shipping, each) of

Those Marvelous Church Suppers

to:
Name: _____

Address: _____

City or Town: _____Prov: _____Postal Code: _____

My cheque or money order for _____ is enclosed.

Mail to:
Wood Lake Books, Inc.   or Those Marvelous Church Suppers
Box 700   Box 8066, Station F,
Winfield, BC,   Edmonton, AB,
V0H 2C0   T6H 4N9

A delightful way to share...

Please send _____ copies (at 12^{95}, plus $1 shipping, each) of

Those Marvelous Church Suppers

to:
Name: _____

Address: _____

City or Town: _____Prov: _____Postal Code: _____

My cheque or money order for _____ is enclosed.

Mail to:
Wood Lake Books, Inc.   or Those Marvelous Church Suppers
Box 700   Box 8066, Station F,
Winfield, BC,   Edmonton, AB,
V0H 2C0   T6H 4N9

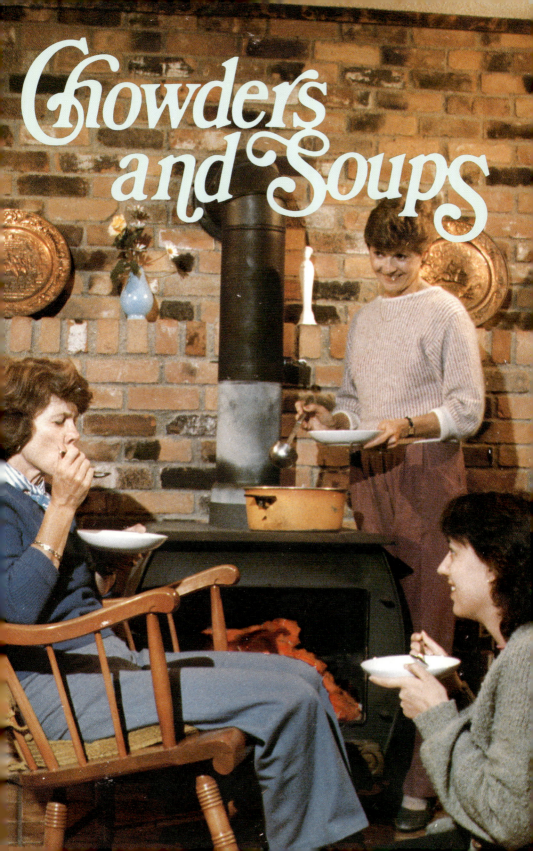

A grace...

*Creator God,
the signs of your love
are all around us;
in the golden energy of a dandelion,
in the tears of a hurting child,
in the love of a caring parent,
in the good food which is before us.
We thank you for the kindness and the skill
of the ones who prepared this food,
and for the caring and the friendship
of those with whom we share it.
May the food and the fellowship
strengthen our lives
that we may be faithful agents
of your justice
and your love
throughout the world.
Amen.*

This recipe was sent by a man who remembers the suppers in the Catholic church in Baie Comeau, Quebec—none other than Canada's Prime Minister, Brian Mulroney. His recipe is for a clear, savory soup which is nice as an appetizer or served with a salad and sandwich.

Brian Mulroney's
Veal Sour Soup

1	**veal knuckle** or shank	1
10 cups	**water**	2.5 L
	salt, to taste	
½ tsp	**peppercorns**	2 mL
2	**fresh tomatoes** chopped	2
1	**medium potato** peeled & chopped	1
1	**onion**, sliced	1
1	**celery** stalk, coarsely chopped	1
1	**green pepper**, coarsely chopped	1
2-3	**cauliflowerets**, coarsely chopped	2-3
¼ cup	**vegetable oil**	60 mL
2 Tbsp	**flour**	30 mL
½ tsp	**paprika**	2 mL
½	**lemon**, juice	½
2 Tbsp	**sour cream**	30 mL

Makes 10 servings.

Place veal knuckle in a large saucepan or soup kettle, add water, bring to a boil & cook, uncovered, 20 minutes. Skim off foam, then reduce heat & add salt to taste, peppercorns, tomatoes, potato and onion. Cover & simmer over low heat 1 hour. Add celery, green pepper & cauliflower.

Prepare roux by blending oil, flour & paprika in a small saucepan over medium heat. Do not brown. Add to soup & boil 10-15 minutes.

Remove veal shank & chop meat. Strain soup into a saucepan, then pour very slowly into a tureen containing blended lemon juice & sour cream. Discard vegetables in strainer. Stir chopped veal into soup & serve.

Almost everyone knows that the Rt. Rev. Robert Smith, Moderator of the United Church of Canada, is a first-class story teller. Few people know that he also excels as a cook. Since he's from Vancouver, it's appropriate that he would contribute "something fishy" to use his words.

The base for this fish soup is light and extremely tasty. You can vary the seafood to suit your family's tastes. The recipe can be easily halved.

Photo: Berkeley Studio

Bob Smith's Cioppino

¼ cup	**olive oil**	60 mL
2	**garlic cloves**, minced	2
1	**medium onion** minced	1
8 cups	**chicken stock**	2 L
28 oz	**canned tomatoes**	796 mL
½ cup	**fresh parsley** chopped	125 mL
¼ tsp	**dried basil**	1 mL
¼ tsp	**thyme**	1 mL
3	**hot pepper sauce**, drops	3
1	**lemon**	1
½ cup	**dry white wine**	125 mL
½ tsp	**salt**	2 mL
¼ tsp	**pepper**	1 mL
1 lb	**fish fillets**, (sole, cod or haddock, fresh or frozen)	450 g
12	**fresh shrimp** or **prawns** (large)	12
12	**fresh clams** scrubbed	12

Makes 8-10 servings.

Allow fillets to thaw if frozen.

In large cooking pot, heat olive oil. Add garlic cloves & onion & saute over low heat till tender. Add chicken stock, canned tomatoes (broken up), parsley, basil, thyme, hot pepper sauce, juice squeezed from the lemon, wine, salt & pepper. Bring to a boil, reduce heat & simmer for ¾ hour.

Bring to a boil again, add clams & sole. When clams are opened, add shrimp & cook for 2 more minutes (longer cooking will toughen fresh shrimp).

If you would rather not have any shellfish, simply increase the amount of fillets! Be sure & buy your seafood from a reputable fish shop; they are usually free with information.

Tester's Hint: Allow clams to soak for about 2 hours in cold *salt* water to which has been added a small handful of rolled oats; this will "encourage" the clams to get rid of any sand!

A toast:
To our best friends,
Who know the worst about us,
But who love us anyway.

Anne Nightingale of Okanagan Centre, B.C., one of the editors of this cookbook, simply had to include this one because it is such a favorite with her family and friends. Besides, it's hearty and tasty, and it can be prepared in very short order.

Anne Nightingale's Hamburger Soup

1 lb	**lean ground beef**	450 g
5 cups	**water**	1.25 L
2 cups	**tomatoes**, canned	500 mL
1 cup	**onions**, chopped	250 mL
4	**carrots**, diced	4
⅓ cup	**barley**	85 mL
¼ cup	**ketchup**	60 mL
1 tsp	**salt**	5 mL
½ tsp	**basil**	2 mL
2	**bay leaves**	2
¼ tsp	**pepper**	1 mL
14 oz	**pork & beans**, can	398 mL
1½ cups	**cabbage**, shredded	375 mL
	sour cream, garnish	

Makes 8 servings.

In a large pot, brown ground beef. Drain off fat.

Add water, then all remaining ingredients. Bring soup to a boil, then reduce heat to a simmer & cook, covered, about 1 hour. Remove bay leaves before serving.

Ladle into bowls & add a dollop of sour cream, if desired.

Photo: Berkeley Studio

If you want a soup that's a meal in itself, try a chowder.

Elizabeth Funge, a member of the United Church Women of Collingwood, P.E.I. (whose picture appears on this page) sent us a recipe similar to this one by Dan Bailey of Wolfville, N.S. This easy fish chowder may be doubled or tripled if you have a crowd or want to serve it to a church group as a welcome change from the usual sweet things.

Dan Bailey's Maritime Fish Chowder

2 Tbsp	**butter**	30 mL
2 med.	**onions**, chopped	2 med.
⅔ cup	**celery**, diced	170 mL
½	**green pepper**, diced	½
2 cups	**boiling water**	500 mL
2 cups	**potatoes**, diced	500 mL
⅔ cup	**carrots**, diced	170 mL
½ tsp	**salt**	2 mL
1/8 tsp	**pepper**	.5 mL
1 lb	**haddock**, fresh or frozen	450 g
2 cups	**canned milk**	500 mL

Makes 6 servings.

Melt butter in large, heavy saucepan & add onions, celery, & green pepper. Cook over low heat till tender. Add water, potatoes, carrots, salt & pepper. Simmer, covered, 10-15 minutes or until vegetables are tender.

Cut haddock into bite-sized pieces. Add to pot & cook 10 more minutes. Add canned milk. Reheat, but do not boil.

Chowders and Soups — 35

"This is right from the home of the clams," says Laura Phillips. From her home in Arlington, P.E.I., she sent us this simple cream-style chowder.

Laura Phillips' Clam Chowder

½ cup	**carrots**, peeled & chopped	125 mL
1 cup	**potato**, peeled & diced	250 mL
¼ cup	**celery**, diced	60 mL
1 small	**onion**, chopped	1 small
¼ tsp	**salt**	1 mL
10 oz	**clams**, tin	284 g
2 Tbsp	**butter**	30 mL

Makes 4 servings.

Combine prepared vegetables in a saucepan. Drain the liquid from the clams into the vegetables & simmer until vegetables are tender.

Chop clams & add to vegetables along with milk, butter & salt. Heat & serve.

Prejudiced against scalloped potatoes...

There's a rumor in some circles that Hugh McCullum, Editor of the *United Church Observer*, is prejudiced.

It's true. He's prejudiced against ham and scalloped potatoes. Hugh explains why.

"*The Observer* has a time-honored tradition of meeting in about 40 Presbyteries a year. These meetings usually involve lunch and supper in church basements catered to by the United Church Women and paid for by the magazine.

"The meals are generally bountiful and delicious. But a couple of years ago, ham must have been available at a very good price. Across Manitoba, Saskatchewan and Alberta in early April we had 10 meetings—five lunches and five suppers. Count 'em. 10 meals, all with ham, scalloped potatoes and mixed peas and carrots. All in five days.

"Home to mother's for Easter. 'A treat, I've got for you for Easter dinner.' I blanched. You guessed it.

"Yes, I am prejudiced.

"But those homemade church basement pies! Now that's another matter!"

Margaret Laurence, one of Canada's most loved and respected writers, loves many things, including hungry teenagers. When her own kids were at that super-hungry stage and constantly bringing their friends home, Margaret invented this soup because it is inexpensive, tasty and filling.

Margaret's soup was tested for this cookbook by the cooking class at the George Elliot High School in Winfield, B.C. On the first try, the young man making the soup had a bit of trouble. He didn't like the results and neither did the teacher.

"What'll we do with all that soup?" she asked.

"Feed it to the grade eights," came the reply. "There's too many of them anyway."

Actually, the soup is quite easy to make and very tasty.

Photo: Doug Bolt

Margaret Laurence's Cauliflower Soup

1	**cauliflower**, med.	1
2	**carrots**, large	2
½ lb	**mushrooms**, fresh	225 g
1	**onion**, chopped	1
	choice of seasonings:	
½ tsp	**worcestershire** sauce	2 mL
¼ tsp	**oregano**, dried	1 mL
½ tsp	**basil**, dried	2 mL
1 Tbsp	**dill weed**, fresh or frozen	15 mL
½ tsp	**dill seed**	2 mL
2 qts	**milk**	2 L
2 cups	**cheddar cheese**, sharp, grated	500 mL

Makes 10-12 servings.

Break cauliflower into flowerets & put in a *large* soup pot. Cook with enough water to barely cover until fork tender. Do not drain. Mash with potato masher.

Grate or dice carrots & add to pot with sliced mushrooms, onions & your choice of seasonings. Add milk; cover & bring to a slow boil, watching carefully. Reduce heat & simmer for an hour.

Add grated cheese* & heat gently about 10 minutes longer. Serve with brown bread.

*We recommend sprinkling grated cheese on soup when served, rather than adding it to the soup pot; croutons would be a nice addition. Texture can be varied by blending all or part of soup.

Amused at their naive mother...

Author Margaret Laurence, of Lakefield, Ontario, remembers those church suppers.

"My memories of church suppers when I was a kid are vivid and warm. In our part of the world they were called 'Fowl Suppers' because there were quantities of chicken and turkey, with marvelous sage and onion stuffing, and lashings of gravy. I seem to recall that there would be roasts of beef as well, but I can't be certain.

"Good grief! Can they have been called 'Fall Suppers'?

"No, I don't think so. Those of us who had an ear for a pun would gleefully say to one another, 'You going to the Church Supper? I bet it'll be *foul*... ha, ha, ha!'

"Of course, we loved those suppers. I doubt that the most expensive restaurants anywhere could put on a better meal than those prepared by the women of the United Church in Neepawa, Manitoba.

"A curious thing is that this was during the Thirties and the Depression, but there certainly was no lack of food. Of course, southern Manitoba never suffered a total crop failure as Saskatchewan did. Also everyone chipped in.

"I recall the pies—every known variety—pumpkin with loads of whipped cream, apple, raisin, lemon meringue...

"My Mum used to contribute apple pies for which she was justly famous, and possibly her delectable Lemon Slice or Thimble Cookies, which were rich, white, shortbread-like cookies with a dint in the middle. You rolled the cookie dough into little balls in your hands, and then donned a thimble on your middle finger and pressed a dint into each cookie. And when they were baked, you filled the dint with homemade strawberry jam or wild pinchberry jelly or whatever was your specialty in the line of preserves.

"The suppers were held in the basement room of the United Church. This largish room also was where the Sunday School met. Dozens of us kids would be running around refilling our plates.

"These were truly family occasions. The kids were as welcome as the adults and we felt a real part of the event. Of course, we didn't analyze it. We just enjoyed it.

"My only sad memory—well, not so much sad as kind of pathetic in retrospect—was of a Sunday School picnic that had to be held in the church basement instead of outdoors for reasons I can't recall.

"I must have been no more than six years old. My Mum had taught me never to take a second sandwich until the first was completely eaten, and not to take a cookie until the sandwiches had been duly consumed. She was not, I hasten to say, a real stickler for etiquette, but she was determined, rightly, that her kids would grow up with good manners.

"I am sure she never foresaw my predicament at that luckless picnic. I took a sandwich when they were passed around and woe! It was peanut butter!

"I loathed peanut butter (I still do). So that was all I got that day. One totally uneaten peanut butter sandwich.

"I never told my Mum. I was ashamed at not being able to choke down the hated sandwich.

"When my own kids were quite young and peanut butter sandwiches their top favorites, I'd tell them this little story. They were amused and yet sorry for that naive kid their mother had been so long ago."

It can get pretty chilly in Fort McMurray, Alberta, which may be why Ron Warrington likes this soup in winter when broccoli is one of the few green vegetables available. It's a beautiful color of green and has a rich flavor.

Ron Warrington's
Cream of Broccoli Soup

3	**broccoli** stalks	3
1	**onion**	1
1	**garlic clove**	1
2½ cups	**chicken stock**	625 mL
3 Tbsp	**butter**	45 mL
3 Tbsp	**flour**	45 mL
2 cups	**whipping cream**	500 mL
	salt, to taste	
	pepper, to taste	
1 tsp	**curry powder**	5 mL

Makes 4 servings.

Pare & chop broccoli, onion & garlic; place in saucepan & add water to cover. Cook until softened. Drain, reserving liquid. Process vegetables in blender with some of the reserved liquid until pureed.

Combine pureed vegetables & chicken stock in large saucepan & keep warm.

In another large saucepan, make a roux by melting the butter & stirring in the flour. Add the whipping cream slowly, stirring constantly. Add salt, pepper & curry.

Now slowly add the warm broccoli mixture to the cream sauce, stirring as you do. Use more of the reserved vegetable cooking liquid to thin the soup if desired.

A more delicately flavored version of this soup can be made by substituting a grating of nutmeg for the curry.

McClure leaped to his feet...

Donna Sinclair of North Bay, Ontario, author of *Worth Remembering*, has found many church suppers worth remembering.

"The church supper I remember best had Dr. Bob McClure as the guest speaker for St. Andrew's Anniversary dinner in 1984.

"Somone complimented the person who had organized the supper. 'Well,' she replied, pointing to the coffee pot in her hand, 'if I'd been better organized, I'd have found somebody else to pour the coffee.'

"McClure leaped to his feet, took the pot, and went from table to table pouring coffee and visiting with a lot of delighted admirers. He was 84, and had already put in a full day of interviews, speeches and appearances."

As her name implies, Melody Drewlo of Winfield, B.C., is very musical, and enjoys singing everything from old hymns to new musicals. Her delicious Gazpacho can be made by substituting frozen or canned tomatoes for the fresh. That way you can enjoy this chilled Spanish soup all year round.

Melody Drewlo's Gazpacho

1	**garlic clove**	1
1	**onion**, chopped	1
2	**cucumbers**, chopped	2
2	**tomatoes**, peeled & chopped	2
½	**green pepper**, chopped	½
14 oz	**tomato sauce**, can	398 mL
10 oz	**consomme**, can	284 mL
¼ cup	**wine vinegar**	60 mL
⅓ cup	**olive oil**	85 mL
¼ tsp	**hot pepper sauce**	1 mL
1 tsp	**salt**	5 mL
	black pepper, to taste	
	croutons	
	cheddar cheese, grated	

Makes 8 servings.

Rub glass bowl with cut clove of garlic. Combine chopped vegetables & pour into seasoned bowl.

Mix together tomato sauce, consomme, vinegar, olive oil, pepper sauce, salt & freshly ground black pepper. Pour over vegetables in bowl. Chill well before serving.

At serving time pass croutons & grated cheese as toppings for soup.

I'm glad to be alive...

The people who do all the hard work at church suppers don't always get all the thanks they deserve. Sometimes they get a bit more than they want.

Rev. Glen Baker of Kelowna, recalls a story from his father, also a minister. Glen's father had asked another minister to give the traditional "thanks to the ladies". The man was a bit bombastic about it all.

"Ladies, after partaking of the abundant repast which you set before us, all I can say is that I'm glad to be alive."

There was a long silence. Then they almost blew the roof off; they laughed so hard.

This soup may well be illegal in Russia where "chilled borsch" might be a contradiction in terms. Anybody with a bit of Ukraine in their blood knows that borsch must be piping hot. That doesn't seem to concern Elaine Towgood of Oyama, B.C., one of the editors of this book. She enjoys this frigid dish, especially in the summer. It's prepared in a blender, which is probably another heresy for traditional borsch lovers.

Elaine Towgood's Chilled Oyama Borsch

2 cups	**cooked beets**, diced	500 mL	
1 cup	**sour cream**, divided	250 mL	
¼ cup	**onion**, chopped	60 mL	
1	**lemon** slice, rind removed	1	
2 Tbsp	**green pepper**, chopped	30 mL	
½ tsp	**sugar**	2 mL	
¼ tsp	**salt**	1 mL	
1 cup	**crushed ice**	250 mL	
4 tsp	**fresh parsley**, chopped	20 mL	

Makes 4 servings.

Into blender container put beets, ¾ cup (180 mL) sour cream, onion, lemon, green pepper, sugar & salt. Blend for 20 seconds.

Add crushed ice & blend. Serve in soup bowls, garnish with a dollop of sour cream & a sprinkle of parsley.

The sharing warms the heart...
Muriel Jones, who is Registrar at St. Stephen's College in Edmonton, sends this delightful, and very recent memory:

"This year, our Church had a Valentine Dance and Box Supper. Very few attended. Some did not bring a box supper.

"A disaster?

"Certainly not! Instead of many tables seating four each, we made one huge square table at one end of the room. Everyone sat around, conversed, became acquainted, danced, sang, and when suppertime arrived we had a grand opening of Valentine-decorated boxes, set out all the goodies in an attractive fashion and shared a splendid feast. Not only was there enough to go around, but some to spare.

"In a spirit of well-being and friendship we reluctantly parted at the close of the evening. My thoughts were of Jesus and the miracle of the loaves and fishes, and how the act of sharing warms the heart. My husband and I drove home feeling that same warmth in our hearts."

Like many ethnic dishes, Pluma Moos (which would loosely translate as "plum paste") developed in the hard days of winter in Canada, and before that in Russia, when dried fruit was all that was available.

This recipe was submitted by Ralph Milton, who (in spite of his name) is a Mennonite boy born in Altona, Manitoba. He is also the Publisher of Wood Lake Books and the author of several books including *Through Rose-Colored Bifocals*.

Pluma Moos was a traditional Easter dish in his family, and is great with smoked ham and freshly baked buns.

Photo: Bob Greichen

Ralph Milton's Pluma Moos

4 cups	dried fruit such as: **prunes, raisins, apples, apricots, pears**	1 L	
2 Tbsp	**flour**	30 mL	
¼ cup	**sugar**	60 mL	
¼ tsp	**cinnamon** or **anise seed**	1 mL	

Makes about 8 servings.

Place dried fruit in a cooking pot & cover with warm water. Let stand for an hour or two. Simmer for about 10 minutes until fruit is tender.

Mix the flour with enough water to make a paste & add this to the fruit. Simmer until thickened, then remove from heat. Add the sugar & cinnamon.

Serve hot as a main course, or better still, allow to cool. Add milk as necessary to "loosen it up a little."

Variations: You can use almost any combination of fruit, even canned or fresh if you want, although canned fruit tends to go soft. You can leave out the sugar &/or the cinnamon if you prefer a more tart & fruity taste.

A recipe for toast...
Dr. Bob Hatfield of Calgary, co-author of *Matters of Life and Death*, sent us the following recipe:

"Place one slice of bread in toaster. Toast until bread is golden brown. Spread on thin layer of butter or margarine, followed by thin layer of jam. Serves one."

Without anxious mothers to check...

"Memories of the CGIT (The Canadian Girls in Training) are warm and strong from many Canadian women," says Rev. John Shearman of Palermo, Ontario. But there's one very special memory that comes from Ottawa during the second World War.

"Many CGIT leaders were young women who had come from across Canada to work in the burgeoning offices of the federal civil service. Because these government girls lived in very meagre rooms, usually without kitchen privileges, it was a rare treat for them to taste a home-cooked meal. CGIT provided the happy exception.

"First United, in the heart of Ottawa's boarding house district, would open its doors to the CGIT girls who would come straight from school to begin preparing supper on their own. When the leaders arrived after work, they would find the tables set, the meal ready and an excited group of girls waiting eagerly for the food to be sampled and approved.

"It was the freedom of the kitchen they enjoyed most. Without anxious mothers to check on what was going on, and with enthusiastic leaders encouraging them, these girls were more than willing to try new adventures in food preparation. This was freedom worth fighting for."

A grace...

*God, our Creator,
you have created the food on this table,
as you have created us.
As loving hands took the fruit you created
in field and farm,
and prepared it for our joy and nourishment,
so we take the lives you have created,
and prepare them for your joy
and for your service.
Help us to be deeply thankful
for the creative life expressed in this food;
the creative love expressed in this fellowship,
and the creative purpose
that is your gift
to each one of us.
Amen.*

For those who find too much food "goes to waist", here's a helping hand from Brian Jackson, one of the ministers at Trinity United in Vernon, B.C.

Brian has invented a salad seasoning that can be used in combination with other dressings, but makes a fine low-cal dressing when used with raw or cooked vegetables. Brian suggests a bit of this seasoning on vegetables done in a microwave, and our recipe testers found it was delightful when sprinkled on chicken pieces before baking.

Brian Jackson's
Salad Seasoning

½ tsp	**paprika**	2 mL	
½ tsp	**garlic powder**	2 mL	
½ tsp	**dry mustard**	2 mL	
5 tsp	**onion powder**	25 mL	
½ tsp	**black pepper**	2 mL	
¼ tsp	**celery seed**	1 mL	

Mix together & store in a covered jar.

Sprinkle on vegetables or salads; takes the place of salt & pepper.

For a low-cal salad, use this in place of an oil dressing.

Boil everything until it's warm...
Many well-known church leaders were asked to contribute recipes for this book. One of them, William Davis who heads the Division of Finance of the United Church, sent this note:

"When forced into the kitchen, I boil everything in water till it is warm and then I eat it. I don't know a single recipe, unless you count cutting lettuce, tomatoes, celery, carrots and radishes into pieces and pouring salad dressing on it."

Here are two delightful dressings from the Okanagan Valley. Bev Ashbaugh of Vernon offers a tasty Italian favorite, and Gladys Perkins of Kelowna contributes a creamy and tangy tomato dressing. Both are well worth trying.

Bev Ashbaugh's
Italian Cheese Dressing

1⅓ cups	**salad oil**	335 mL
½ cup	**vinegar**	125 mL
⅓ cup	**parmesan cheese**, grated	85 mL
1 Tbsp	**sugar**	15 mL
2 tsp	**salt**	10 mL
1 tsp	**celery salt**	5 mL
½ tsp	**pepper**	2 mL
½ tsp	**dry mustard**	2 mL
¼ tsp	**paprika**	1 mL
1	**garlic clove**, minced	1

Makes 1¾ cup (430 mL).

Put all ingredients into blender container, blend until combined. Chill.

Gladys Perkins'
Tomato Dressing

2 cups	**tomato soup** condensed	500 mL
1 cup	**vegetable oil**	250 mL
1 tsp	**paprika**	5 mL
6 drops	**worcestershire sauce**	6 drops
3 Tbsp	juice from **pickled onions**	45 mL
¼ cup	chopped **onion**	60 mL
½ cup	**sugar**	125 mL
1 cup	**vinegar**	250 mL
1 tsp	**salt**	5 mL
1 drop	**tabasco sauce**	1 drop

Makes 4½ cups (1 litre).

Process in blender at high speed.

Low calorie variation: substitute ¼ cup (60 mL) artificial sweetener for the sugar.

Salads and Veggies — 47

Elaine Towgood, when testing this recipe, didn't realize that mustard seed pops like corn. She got it all over her kitchen floor, which is why there's a suggestion in the recipe about using a screen.

The recipe comes from Paula Locke of University Hill United in Vancouver. It's a salad with quite a difference and an intriguing flavor.

Photo: Bob Greichen

Paula Locke's Gujerati Carrot Salad

¾ lb	**carrots**, grated coarsely	340 g
¼ tsp	**salt**	1 mL
2 tsp	**lemon juice**	10 mL
2 Tbsp	**sultana raisins** (optional)	30 mL
2 Tbsp	**vegetable oil**	30 mL
1 Tbsp	**mustard seeds**, whole, black*	15 mL

The mustard seeds pop like corn—be ready to move fast when they begin to pop! Use a screen over the pot.

Makes 6-8 servings.

In a bowl, toss carrots with salt, lemon juice & raisins.

Heat the oil in a small saucepan over medium heat until very hot. Add the mustard seed. When the seeds begin to pop, pour contents over the carrot mixture.

You may serve this salad at room temperature or cold.

*Yellow mustard seed may be used if the black ones are unavailable.

A walking salad for travelling Christians...

Church suppers don't necessarily happen around long tables with white table cloths. Here's a bit of remembering from Mardi Tindal, on the staff of the Hamilton Conference of the United Church.

"The most wonderful church suppers were those shared at church camp—from the rowdy dining hall feasts to the crunchy, buggy, often-burnt but always succulent, campfire meals.

"There's one I remember particularly. The day was warm, sunny and green when our little group hit the trail for an all-day hike. When it came time to share lunch, the 'tripper' pulled two ingredients out of a knapsack. 'We're going to have walking salad', she announced.

"The two ingredients were cabbage and peanut butter. Each person took a cabbage leaf, spread it with peanut butter, rolled it up and had their first of many servings of 'walking salad'. I think I remember it more for the conversation than for the taste.

"We talked about 'walking salad' being an appropriate kind of meal for travelling Christians. It was simple, nutritious, and fun, *and* it didn't take us off the trail for long. After all, we had a lot of ground to cover."

Rev. Bev Milton would heap her plate full of this salad at every potluck supper in the Winfield United Church. Now, after some brilliant detective work, she finally found the recipe. It belonged to Kay Taylor.

This salad is a deliciously different blending of flavors and textures, and is particularly suited to summertime suppers. You can add a bit of color and interest by putting in some cauliflower or broccoli.

Kay Taylor's
Marinated Carrot Salad

10 oz	**tomato soup**, canned	284 mL
1 cup	**sugar** (may be reduced)	250 mL
½ cup	**vinegar**	125 mL
½ cup	**cooking oil**	125 mL
1 tsp	**worcestershire sauce**	5 mL
1 tsp	**dry mustard**	5 mL
	salt, to taste	
4 cups	**carrots**, sliced in rounds	1 L
1	**green pepper**, cut in strips	1
1	**onion**, sliced in rings	1

In a small saucepan, combine tomato soup, sugar, vinegar, cooking oil, worcestershire sauce, dry mustard & salt. Bring to the boil & remove from heat.

Cook carrots in a small amount of water for 5 minutes. Drain & combine with green pepper & onion rings. Pour the vinegar mixture over the vegetables & chill till serving time in a covered bowl.

This recipe was contributed by Chimaki Kamakura, a warm and unassuming person whom many people will remember for her great contribution to the church in western Canada. Before she retired to her family home in Japan, she left this delightful recipe.

When researching and testing it, Elaine and Anne found that one kind of Sunomono is made with thin white noodles, cucumber and vinegar. This version, however, calls for cabbage and cucumber marinated in vinegar. It's pleasant at any meal.

Chimaki Kamakura's Sunomono (Japanese Salad)

½	**cabbage**, firm head	½
1	**cucumber**, peeled	1
1 tsp	**salt**	5 mL
1 Tbsp	**sugar**	15 mL
¾ cup	**rice vinegar**	180 mL
4	**radishes**, sliced	4

Makes 8 servings.

Shred cabbage as finely as possible; cut peeled cucumber paper thin. Put both in a glass or china bowl. Sprinkle salt over all & allow vegetables to sit for about 2 hours. Squeeze out any accumulated juice & discard.

Combine sugar & rice vinegar (milder tasting than regular vinegar) & pour over vegetables. Sprinkle thinly-sliced radish over top for color.

This salad may be served cooled or at room temperature.

To keep their minds off the delectable smells

Rhoda Playfair Stein is Editor of *B.C. Image,* a magazine of the United Church in B.C. That task takes her to many church suppers, and sometimes brings back memories.

"I remember the old 'fowl suppers' held in the basement of St. Thomas-Wesley United Church in Saskatoon.

"There were always two sittings, with entertainment in the sanctuary to help those of us gathered for the second sitting keep our minds off the delectable smells wafting up the stairway. When at last we wound our way down (past the early eaters with satisfied smiles winding their way up), there were the tables groaning with huge bowls and platters of food prepared on two wood stoves in an incredibly hot, tiny kitchen by the ladies of the Women's Auxiliary.

"I've attended lots of church suppers, but none of them have tasted quite as good as that."

Those Marvelous Church Suppers

Few people are as busy as Muriel Duncan, the Managing Editor of the United Church Observer. After long hours at the office, she still manages some creative cooking.

The banana in this cabbage salad gives it a mildly sweet flavor which is really tasty.

Muriel Duncan's Genevieve's Salad

DRESSING:

1½ tsp	**prepared mustard**	7 mL
⅓ cup	**sugar**	85 mL
1 tsp	**salt**	5 mL
1	**egg**	1
½ cup	**sweet pickle juice**	125 mL
1 cup	**milk**	250 mL
1 tsp	**butter**	5 mL
	sweet pickle juice for diluting dressing	

Makes 1½ cups (375 mL).

Combine mustard, sugar & salt in top of double boiler; beat in egg with a fork; add pickle juice & stir; add milk & stir.

Cook over boiling water until the sauce thickens enough to coat the spoon. Remove from heat & add butter. Chill.

SALAD:

2 cups	**cabbage**, shredded	500 mL
2 Tbsp	**onion**, diced	30 mL
½	**banana**, diced	½

Makes 4 servings.

Toss together finely shredded cabbage, diced onion & diced banana. Combine some salad dressing & pickle juice in a ratio of 2 parts salad dressing: 1 part pickle juice. Stir thoroughly into vegetables & serve. Store surplus dressing in covered container in refrigerator.

A Jewish toast:

"Lekayyim!" ("To Life!")

This must be a very popular salad, because so many people sent it to us. Some variations add shredded carrots, or green and red peppers which would certainly make it more eye-appealing. It's a large recipe that keeps well in the fridge for several days, which is great if you have lots of people dropping by.

Those sending in this recipe included Viola Manery of Keremeos, B.C., Connie Bickford, who is Church Secretary at the South Burnaby United Church, Florence Parkinson of Kelowna who got it from Mary Klochko of Kamsack, Saskatchewan, and Genevieve Carder of Toronto. Genevieve always takes this to pot luck suppers at St. Matthews United in Toronto, after one memorable occasion when "everybody brought dessert."

Genevieve Carder's Pickled Coleslaw

1 large	cabbage	1 large
2	onions	2
¾ cup	sugar	180 mL
1 tsp	salt	5 mL
1 cup	vinegar	250 mL
2 tsp	prepared mustard	10 mL
¼ cup	sugar	60 mL
1 Tbsp	celery seed	15 mL
¾ cup	salad oil	180 mL

Makes 24 servings.

Shred cabbage finely; chop onions. Place in large bowl with ¾ cup (180 mL) sugar & salt, toss & let stand while preparing the dressing.

Mix the vinegar, prepared mustard, ¼ cup (60 mL) sugar & celery seed in a medium saucepan. Bring to boil, then add salad oil. Pour the hot dressing over shredded vegetables & stir well.

Cover & refrigerate overnight before serving.

Eating philosophy...

Here's a bit of eating "philosophy" from Rev. G.E. Waddell of Newdale, Manitoba.

"I like my eggs
Boiled hard as sin,
So hard they don't
Drip down my chin."

What the eye sees is sometimes as important in cooking as what the tongue tastes. That's why we recommend this salad sent to us by Barbara Ferris of Kelowna, B.C. When it's made in a clear glass bowl, this salad is very attractive. It's made the night before and kept in the fridge till serving time.

Barbara Ferris' Layered Lettuce Salad

1 head	**lettuce**	1 head	
1 cup	**celery**, diced	250 mL	
4	**eggs**, hard boiled	4	
10 oz	**frozen peas**, pkg.	284 g	
½	**green pepper**	½	
1 med	**onion**, sweet	1 med	
8 slices	**bacon**, cooked & crumbled	8 slices	
2 cups*	**mayonnaise**	500 mL	
2 Tbsp	**sugar**	30 mL	
¾ cup	**cheddar cheese**, grated	180 mL	

Makes 10-12 servings.

Tear washed lettuce into bite-sized pieces & put into a large salad bowl. Layer over lettuce the celery, sliced hard-boiled eggs, frozen peas (not thawed), sliced or chopped green pepper, chopped onion & bacon pieces.

Combine mayonnaise (*may be reduced to 1 cup - 250 mL) & sugar in small bowl; "ice" salad with this mixture & top with grated cheese.

Cover dish with plastic wrap & refrigerate for at least 12 hours before serving.

Some salads are almost a meal in themselves. This delicious "caesar" type salad turns a meal into something special. We suggest you toss it with the dressing just before serving. It comes from Margaret Kawano, who lives in Winfield, B.C.

This recipe was specially requested by Bill Davis, who can't cook but loves salads. He heads the Finance Division at United Church headquarters in Toronto.

Margaret Kawano's
Spinach Salad

SALAD:

2 bunches	**spinach**	2 bunches
	or:	
1 head	**romaine lettuce**	1 head
3	**green onions**, chopped	3
½ lb	**mushrooms**, sliced	225 g
½ cup	**Swiss cheese**, grated	125 mL
¼ lb	**bacon**, cooked & crumbled	110 g
3	**eggs**, hard boiled for garnish	3

DRESSING:

1	**egg**	1
1	**garlic clove**, minced	1
1 tsp	**dry mustard**	5 mL
½ tsp	**sugar**	2 mL
dash	**salt**	dash
dash	**pepper**	dash
¾ cup	**salad oil**, divided	180 mL
3 Tbsp	**white wine vinegar**	45 mL
3	**anchovies**, chopped (optional)	3

Makes 8 servings.

Combine washed spinach with green onions, mushrooms, cheese & bacon in salad bowl. Set aside.

Break raw egg into blender container, add garlic clove, mustard, sugar, salt, pepper (& anchovies if using) & ¼ cup (60 mL) of the salad oil. Blend thoroughly. With blender still running, slowly pour remaining ½ cup (125 mL) salad oil through blender top. Lastly blend in vinegar.

Toss dressing with salad ingredients, except eggs; use these to garnish top.

The God of Israel has said, "Let my people go, so that they may keep a feast in the wilderness in honor of me."

Exodus 5:1-2

If you're having a bunch of people over for a meal, try this potato salad that came from Pat McCoubrey, who has taken it to a number of suppers at the United Church in Winfield, B.C. The curry makes this an interesting variation on an old favorite. Some people might like a little less dressing.

Pat McCoubrey's Party Potato Salad

8 cups	**potatoes**, cooked & diced	2 L	
4	**green onions**, chopped	4	
4	**eggs**, hard boiled & chopped	4	
1 tsp	**celery seed**	5 mL	
1½ tsp	**salt**	7 mL	
¼ tsp	**pepper**	1 mL	
1 tsp	**curry powder** (optional)	5 mL	
1 cup	**sour cream**	250 mL	
½ cup	**mayonnaise**	125 mL	
2 Tbsp	**vinegar**	30 mL	
	parsley sprigs garnish		
	paprika - garnish		

Makes about 10 servings.

Mix potatoes, onions, eggs, celery seed, salt & pepper.

Mix curry powder with sour cream. Add mayonnaise & vinegar.

Mix vegetables & dressing together & garnish with parsley & paprika. Chill in refrigerator until serving time.

Here's a delicious main dish salad, that comes from Dianne Friesen of Winfield, B.C. It makes a tasty addition to a summertime buffet.

Photo: Bob Greichen

Dianne Friesen's Macaroni Shrimp Salad

1 lb	**macaroni**	450 g
¼ cup	**radishes**	60 mL
½ cup	**celery**	125 mL
¼ cup	**green pepper**	60 mL
¼ cup	**green onion**	60 mL
2-4 oz	**shrimp**, cans	2-113 g
1¾ cups	**mayonnaise**, divided	430 mL
1 cup	**ketchup**, divided	250 mL

Makes 12 servings.

Boil macaroni according to package directions until tender. Drain & rinse well with cold water.

Chop radishes, celery, green pepper & green onion finely. Add to macaroni.

Drain the shrimp & reserve liquid. Add shrimp to macaroni. Combine liquid with 1¼ cups (310 mL) mayonnaise & ¾ cup (180 mL) ketchup. Stir into salad & refrigerate 3 hours or overnight.

Before serving, stir in remaining ½ cup (125 mL) mayonnaise & ¼ cup (60 mL) ketchup.

Gave the food a kind of radiance...

Dr. Bill Taylor, former principal of Union College in Vancouver, remembers a "marvelous church supper" during his days as a missionary in India.

"It was a small village. It was a poor village too, made even poorer by the fact that they refused to sell in the market on Sunday. They accepted that loss of income cheerfully, knowing that in the process they were also witnessing to their faith.

"We gathered in the little bare, mud-floored, mud-walled, thatch-roofed church. We all sat on the earth floor. The service was led by a veteran missionary, now very old and not at all well, and by a very elderly Indian gentleman.

"These two men talked together of what God had meant in their lives. One was Canadian, one Indian. One highly educated. One illiterate. But in that sharing any walls between them dissolved.

"After the service we had our congregational supper. There were chapattis, the flat, unleavened bread. And rice, vegetable curry and some pilau. But the worship service we had just shared gave even that simple and coarse food a kind of quiet radiance."

This recipe came to us from two clergy families. Rev. Allan and Megumi Saunders of St. Paul's United in Estevan, Saskatchewan, sent it in and so did Rev. Phil and Audrey Cline of Toronto.

Phil is the former General Secretary of the United Church's General Council. Since we've got Phil Cline's photo on this page, but it's Audrey who makes the salad for the suppers at Wilmar Heights United Church, we'll credit the salad to the other three in this foursome.

This salad, by the way, can be served as either a main course or as a desert.

Photo: Berkeley Studio

Megumi, Allan and Audrey's Twenty-four Hour Salad

2	**eggs**	2
¼ cup	**lemon juice**, fresh, frozen or canned	60 mL
¼ cup	**sugar**	60 mL
1/8 tsp	**salt**	.5 mL
1 cup	**whipping cream**, whipped	250 mL
¾ lb	**marshmallows**, miniature or:	340 g
24	**marshmallows**, large, quartered	24
14 oz	**pineapple** chunks, canned	398 mL
10 oz	**mandarin orange** segments, canned or:	284 mL
1 lge	**fresh orange**, peeled & cut up	1 lge
¼ cup	**maraschino cherries**, quartered	60 mL
2 cups	**any other canned or fresh fruit**, pared & cut up	500 mL
½ cup	**almonds**, slivered toasted	125 mL

Makes 12-14 servings.

In double boiler, beat eggs with a fork; stir in lemon juice, sugar & salt. Cook over hot water, stirring 5 mins. or until mixture thickens. Remove from heat; cool.

Fold in whipped cream, marshmallows & fruits. Refrigerate overnight.

Just before serving, fold in toasted almond slivers.

Eat, drink and love; the rest's not worth a fillip.

Byron

Here's another popular recipe that came in various versions from all over B.C.'s Interior. Betty DeBeck, on the management committee of the Kamloops United Church, Athelene Secret of Kelowna, and Dorothy Snodgrass of Westbank all sent it in.

We're crediting it to Florence Anderson of Creston because she has pull; her daughter, Joan Taylor, is one of the owners of Wood Lake Books, publishers of this cookbook.

This is a "loaded" jellied salad which is almost a meal in itself.

Florence Anderson's Lemon Cottage Cheese Salad

6 oz pkg	**gelatin**, lemon-flavored	170 g
1 cup	**boiling water**	250 mL
16 oz	dry **cottage cheese**	450 g
14 oz	**pineapple, crushed** slightly drained	398 mL
1½ cups	**celery**, finely chopped	375 mL
1 cup	**mayonnaise**	250 mL
1 cup	**milk**	250 mL

Dissolve lemon gelatin in boiling water. Cool slightly, then add remaining ingredients. Pour into an oiled 1 qt. (1 L) mold or 8 individual molds & refrigerate until set.

The fruit & vegetables in this jellied salad can be substituted to suit your taste, provided they add up to the same number of cups (mLs).

Photo: Berkeley Studio

Not everyone likes jellied salads, but it's hard to imagine anyone not liking these two delightful dishes from Winfield, B.C.

Lorraine Munro's tangy salad makes a nice accompaniment to roast beef. The second salad comes from Jean Daniels.

Lorraine Munro's Molded Beet Salad

14 oz	**canned beets**, diced	398 mL
3 oz pkg	**gelatin**, lemon-flavored	84 g
¼	**lemon**, peeled & seeded	¼
1 tsp	**salt**	5 mL
¼	**onion**, small	¼
1 Tbsp	**horseradish**	15 mL
2	**carrots**	2

Makes 6 servings.

Drain beets, reserving liquid. Add water to beet juice to make 1 cup (250 mL) & bring to a boil.

Put boiling beet juice & gelatin in blender container; cover & blend on low until gelatin is dissolved. Add lemon, salt, onion & horseradish; cover & blend on high till smooth. Add carrots; cover & blend on low, just until carrots are *coarsely* chopped. Add beets, cover & run on medium just until all beets are chopped.

Pour into a lightly oiled 4 cup (1 L) mold. Chill until set.

Serve on salad greens with mayonnaise.

Jean Daniels' Vegetable Jellied Salad

3 oz pkg.	**lime gelatin**	85 g
1 cup	**boiling water**	250 mL
2 Tbsp	**vinegar**	30 mL
1 Tbsp	prepared **mustard**	15 mL
1 tsp	**salt**	5 mL
1½ cups	**cabbage**, shredded	375 mL
1 cup	**carrots**, grated	250 mL
½ cup	**celery**, chopped finely	125 mL
½ cup	**mayonnaise**	125 mL
½ cup	**sour cream**	125 mL

Makes 6 servings.

Combine gelatin with boiling water, stir till dissolved.

In a small glass mix vinegar, mustard & salt. Stir, then add to gelatin.

Add cabbage, carrots & celery to gelatin mixture.

Combine mayonnaise & sour cream & add to gelatin & vegetables. Stir till well mixed.

Pour into lightly oiled 4-5 cup (approx. 1 L) jelly mold. Chill in fridge till set.

This packed jelly salad will set in about 2-3 hours. A salad "maker" or food processor is a great help for shredding the cabbage.

This recipe, along with a "hopeful" story, came from Rev. Phyllis Barnes of St. Mary's, Ontario. She says this "scrumptious concoction has the added advantage of allowing you to brag about eating vegetarian style (ovo-lacto).

Phyllis took this dish to a potluck supper where her congregation talked through a very difficult problem, about farm families "lost from the farming way of life through no wish of their own, and the unbelieving society around us seems content with the prediction that another 40 percent will be squeezed out over the next few years." But says Phyllis, this is a hopeful story, because people got together to share a common problem, and found a way of "mobilizing our love and faith so that the church will not be bound by feelings of helplessness."

By the way, you can have a delightful vegetarian dinner if you serve this with the marinated carrot salad (which you'll also find in this cookbook) and whole-wheat buns.

Phyllis Barnes' Cheese and Spinach Squares

1 lb	**fresh spinach**	450 g
3	**eggs**	3
6 Tbsp	**whole-wheat flour**	90 mL
½ tsp	**salt**	2 mL
2 cups	**cottage cheese**, creamed	500 mL
2 cups	**cheddar cheese**, grated	500 mL
3 Tbsp	**wheat germ**	45 mL

Makes 10-12 servings.

Preheat oven to 350ºF.

Thoroughly wash spinach, pat dry & chop.

In a *very* large mixing bowl, beat eggs, flour & salt till smooth. Add chopped spinach, cottage cheese & cheddar cheese. Toss lightly till spinach is coated with cheeses.

Pack spinach in a well-greased 9" x 13" (22.5 x 32.5 cm) pan. Sprinkle with wheat germ. Tuck spinach down along sides of dish with rubber spatula. Loosely cover with tin foil.

Bake at 350ºF. for 15 minutes. Remove foil. Continue baking uncovered for another 30 minutes.

Cut into squares & serve hot.

We wondered about the name of this recipe, and puzzled over whether it was a main course, a dessert or a salad. It comes from Chris Shennon of Winfield, B.C. We're not sure if it belongs in the "Salads" category of this cookbook, but it does belong on your table because it's delicious.

Chris Shennon's Broccoli Cheese Squares

2-10 oz	**broccoli**, frozen pkg. or:	2-284 mL
1½ lb	**broccoli**	675 g
3	**eggs**	3
1 cup	**flour**	250 mL
1 cup	**milk**	250 mL
1 tsp	**salt**	5 mL
1 tsp	**baking powder**	5 mL
2 cups	**cheddar cheese**, grated	500 mL
2 Tbsp	**onion**, chopped	30 mL

Makes 12 servings.

Preheat oven to 350°F.

Steam broccoli till tender. Rinse with cold water to stop the cooking & chop in blender, *or* chop finely with a knife.

In a large bowl, beat eggs; add flour, milk, salt & baking powder. Mix thoroughly. Add chopped broccoli, grated cheese & onion & mix well.

Butter a 9" x 13" (22.5 x 32.5 cm) pyrex dish. Spoon broccoli mixture into dish.

Bake at 350°F. for 35 minutes.

It's always nice to have a dish that can be made ahead of time, so you can have a bit of time to enjoy the guests when they arrive. Or treat yourself to a last-minute panic. Either way, you'll appreciate this attractive dish sent to us by Catherine Craig of St. Ann's Catholic Church in Abbotsford, B.C.

Catherine Craig's Vegetable Casserole

3 large	**carrots**	3 large	
1½ lb	**broccoli**	775 g	
1 med	**cauliflower**	1 med	

Serves 8-10.

Day before, slice carrots diagonally, ¼ " (.5 cm) thick. Peel broccoli stems & cut into thin slices. Break cauliflower into flowerets. Break large flowerets in half. Wash vegetables thoroughly & steam till barely tender; plunge into cold water & drain.

SAUCE:
5 Tbsp	**butter**	75 mL
5 Tbsp	**flour**	75 mL
½ tsp	**salt**	2 mL
½ tsp	**pepper**	2 mL
1 Tbsp	**Dijon mustard**	15 mL
2¾ cups	**milk**	680 mL
1½ cups	**cheddar cheese** grated	375 mL
2 Tbsp	**parsley**, chopped	30 mL

Melt butter over medium heat & stir in flour. Add salt, pepper, mustard & combine. Gradually add milk & stir constantly till mixture thickens & boils. Reduce heat & stir in grated cheese & parsley.

Pour half the sauce into 9" x 13" (22.5 x 32.5 cm) casserole dish. Arrange vegetables evenly, top with remaining sauce & coat *lightly*. (If making ahead, cover & refrigerate at this point.)

TOPPING:
2 Tbsp	**butter**	30 mL
1 cup	**dry bread crumbs**	250 mL
⅓ cup	**parmesan cheese**	85 mL
¼ cup	**almonds**, slivered toasted	60 mL

Before baking, combine topping ingredients & sprinkle over vegetables. Bake uncovered at 325°F. for 45 minutes, or till hot & bubbly.

"The regenerate use eating, drinking and clothing and shelter with thanksgiving to support their own lives and to the free service of their neighbor according to the Word of the Lord."

Menno Simons

People who grow gardens know that when you have zucchini, *you have zucchini!* This layered vegetable casserole is a tasty way to serve all that extra zucchini. If you don't have zucchini, try eggplant. If you don't have either, wait till next year.

This came from Joan Prentice who is active at the Dunbar United Church in Vancouver.

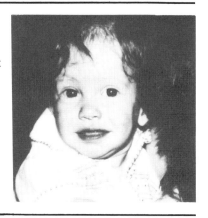

Joan Prentice's Zucchini-Tomato Casserole

1 cup	**cheddar cheese**, grated	250 mL	
⅓ cup	**parmesan cheese**, grated	85 mL	
½ tsp	**oregano**	2 mL	
½ tsp	**basil**	2 mL	
1	**garlic clove**, minced	1	
½ tsp	**salt**	2 mL	
¼ tsp	**pepper**	1 mL	
3	**zucchini**, 10″ (25 cm) long	3	
3	**tomatoes**, medium	3	
¼ cup	**butter**	60 mL	
2 Tbsp	**onion**, chopped finely	30 mL	
½ cup	**dry bread crumbs**	125 mL	

Makes 6 servings.

Preheat oven to 375°F.

Combine cheeses, herbs, garlic, salt & pepper.

Thinly slice zucchini & tomatoes. Butter an 8″ x 8″ (20 x 20 cm) pan.

Arrange half the zucchini slices in pan; then half the tomatoes, sprinkle with half the cheese mixture. Repeat these layers, topping with the cheese.

Melt butter, saute onion in butter until soft. Add crumbs & stir until butter is absorbed. Sprinkle on top of casserole.

Cover loosely & bake at 375°F. for 30 mins. Uncover & bake 20-25 minutes or until topping is crusty & vegetables tender.

I was feeling desperately homesick...

Diane Forrest, author of *The Adventurers*, recently returned from an extensive trip through Asia. One of her experiences showed that those marvelous church suppers happen wherever two or three gather together in faith and love.

"My eating experiences ranged from a wonderful feast in a Chinese home to food poisoning at a Sultan's birthday party. But whether the food was appetizing or appalling, it was always foreign.

"That's one of the reasons I was feeling desperately homesick in Hong Kong. That's when two American Methodist missionaries invited me to lunch.

"Dorothy Jones and Tom Lung have lived in the Far East for more than a quarter of a century, so I expected the meal to be oriental. Instead, it was fresh greens, muffins, and that most North American dish, jellied salad. Their friendship and their food cured my homesickness."

This simple yet unusual casserole makes an interesting accompaniment to "unsauced" dishes like meat loaf or pork chops. It comes from Glenna Christophers, one of the "pillars" of the Winfield United Church Women. Kalamalka is a very lovely lake near Glenna's home. A similar recipe was contributed by Margaret Pursley of Palermo United Church. By the way, this recipe can be halved.

Glenna Christophers' Kalamalka Casserole

4 cups	**canned tomatoes**	1 L
¼ cup	**celery leaves**, chopped	60 mL
1	**medium onion** chopped	1
1	**green pepper**, chopped	1
1 tsp	**sugar**	5 mL
1 tsp	**salt**	5 mL
½ tsp	**pepper**	2 mL
16	**soda crackers**	16
2 tsp	**butter**	10 mL
2 Tbsp	**parmesan cheese**	30 mL

Makes 8 servings.

Preheat oven to 350ºF.

Break up canned tomatoes with a fork & pour into a buttered 6 cup (1.5 L) casserole dish. Add celery leaves, onion & green pepper. Stir in sugar, salt & pepper. Finally, break (do not crush) soda crackers into pieces & stir into vegetables.

Dot the butter over top & sprinkle parmesan cheese over all.

Cover & bake at 350ºF. for 15 minutes. Remove lid & continue baking for another 20 minutes.

Cheryl Doull first tasted these hash potatoes at an Order of St. Luke supper meeting in Brandon, Manitoba. "Then my mother brought the same recipe home from her nondenominational church in Texas where she spends her winters. Small world!"

Cheryl is active at St. Paul's United Church in Souris, Manitoba.

A similar recipe was sent to us by Pat Litke of Campbell-Stone Church in Calgary.

This large quantity potato dish is quick and easy to make with delicious results. And it's easily reheated.

Cheryl Doull's St. Luke Potatoes

½ cup	**butter**, melted	125 mL
2 cups	**sour cream**	500 mL
2-10 oz	**mushroom soup**, cans	2-284 mL
2	**onions**, grated	2
2 cups	**cheddar cheese**, grated	500 mL
	salt & **pepper**, to taste	
2 lb	frozen **hash brown potatoes**	900 g
½ cup	**parmesan cheese**	125 mL

Makes about 12 servings.

Preheat oven to 350ºF.

Mix butter, sour cream, soup, onion, cheddar cheese, salt & pepper. Pour this over the potatoes.

Spoon into a greased 9" x 13" (22.5 x 32.5cm) casserole & sprinkle parmesan cheese over top. Bake at 350ºF. for 1½-2 hours.

An Irish toast:

"And may you be half an hour in heaven before the devil knows you're dead."

Ron and Kris Klusmeier claim an unofficial record for having eaten more of those marvelous church suppers "in more different places than anyone in North America." Ron and Kris are well-known across this country and in the U.S.A. for their fine Christian music. They've presented concerts in every province, and probably *have* eaten more church suppers than anyone.

So how do they keep looking so slim? It probably has nothing to do with this salad, which got top marks from our tasting panel. It's a natural to serve with the best wurst, or with fried chicken.

Photo: Hugo Redivo

Ron & Kris Klusmeier's
German Potato Salad

8-10	**potatoes**	8-10
1	**onion**, sliced thin	1
6	**bacon** slices	6
⅓ cup	**sugar**	85 mL
1 tsp	**salt**	5 mL
dash	**pepper**	dash
½ tsp	**dry mustard** (optional)	2 mL
2 Tbsp	**flour**	30 mL
½ cup	**vinegar**	125 mL
1 cup	**water**	250 mL
	parsley, chopped - garnish	

Makes 8-10 servings.

Cook potatoes *just* until fork tender. Cool. Peel & dice potatoes into a bowl, add onion slices.

In a large skillet, brown the bacon. Remove from pan, reserving fat, & crumble into potato mixture.

Combine sugar, salt, pepper, mustard & flour. Add vinegar & water, mix, then pour into bacon fat in skillet. Cook, stirring until thickened.

Add potato mixture to the skillet & gently stir to coat potatoes with the dressing. Sprinkle with parsley if desired. Serve warm.

The idea of a hot salad may be new to many of us, but this one is certainly worth trying. Pat McCoubrey of Winfield sent in one version, but the one you see here came from Diane Forrest of Toronto, who is the author of *The Adventurers*, a book of stories about Christians who lived their faith.

This is an unusual, but a very tasty casserole. Not only is it served hot, but is also *hot* as in spicy. If you have a delicate palate, just cut back on the peppers. The recipe can be easily halved.

Diane Forrest's Hot Rice Salad

1	**onion**, chopped	1
¼ cup	**butter**	60 mL
4 cups	**cooked rice**	1 L
2 cups	**sour cream**	500 mL
1 cup	**cottage cheese**	250 mL
½ tsp	**basil**, dried	2 mL
	salt & pepper, to taste	
1 cup	*****hot banana peppers**, chopped	250 mL
2 cups	**cheddar cheese** grated	500 mL
	parsley, garnish	

Makes 8-10 servings.

Preheat oven to 375°F.

Saute onion in butter till tender. Add cooked rice, sour cream, cottage cheese, crushed basil, salt & pepper. Stir together & heat through.

Spoon half of the rice mixture into a shallow buttered casserole dish—9" x 13" (22.5 x 32.5 cm). Layer half the chopped peppers & half the cheese over rice. Repeat layers.

Bake at 375°F. for 30 minutes.

Serve hot, garnished with parsley.

*Banana peppers can be found in the pickle section of the grocery store, but watch as they come in "sweet" or "hot", and it's the hot you want for this recipe.

Invite the poor, the crippled...

"When you give a lunch or a dinner, do not invite your friends or your family or your relatives or your rich neighbors—for they will invite you back and in this way you will be paid for what you did.

"When you give a feast, invite the poor, the crippled, the lame, and the blind, and you will be blessed, because they are not able to pay you back."

Luke 14: 12,13

Laura Hawthorn of Bracebridge, Ontario, sent us a lot of recipes. It's too bad we didn't have room for all of them.

But we wouldn't have missed this one, which has a variety of flavors and textures. It's very tasty.

Laura Hawthorn's Wild Rice Casserole

½ cup	**wild rice** or **brown rice** or combination	125 mL
2¼ cups	**boiling water**	560 mL
½ cup	**rice, long grain**	125 mL
3 Tbsp	**butter**	45 mL
1 cup	**onion**, chopped	250 mL
1 cup	**celery**, sliced diagonally	250 mL
½ lb	**mushrooms**, fresh or canned	225 g
¼ cup	**soy sauce**	60 mL
7 oz	**water chestnuts**, canned	227 mL
⅓ cup	**slivered almonds** toasted	85 mL
¾ cup	**dry bread crumbs**	180 mL
2 Tbsp	**butter**, melted	30 mL

Makes 8 servings.

Preheat oven to 350°F.

Add washed wild or brown rice to boiling water; cover, reduce heat & simmer 20 minutes. Add white rice, bring to boil, reduce heat & simmer 20 minutes longer.

Melt butter in frying pan over medium heat & saute onion, celery & mushrooms till tender. Combine with cooked rice, soy sauce & sliced water chestnuts. Spoon into buttered 7-cup (approx. 2 L) casserole dish.

Mix almonds with crumbs & melted butter; sprinkle over rice.

Bake at 350°F. for 30 minutes.

Jay Howarth's recipe for a Bologna Sandwich;

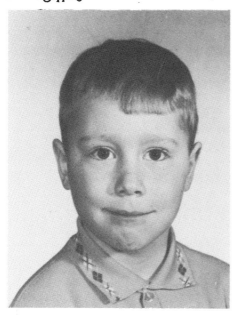

> balonie samwich
> two - slices of bread white + brown
> one - slice of balonie.
> mustard, apple + straberry jam
> white sugar.
>
> Jay's own recipe - age 7

Jay wrote that recipe when he was seven. He was a healthy lad, who loved food in general and church suppers in particular. For most of his life, he sang in the boys' choir at All Saints' Anglican Church in Winnipeg, often helping to serve the meals at many church events, and always enjoying the food and the people.

Jay died at the age of 22, after a long battle with cancer. This recipe was sent to us by his mother.

A grace...

*God of our mothers and fathers,
we thank you for the faith
handed down into our keeping
and into our living.
We thank you for an ancient faith
that gives power to our lives
and meaning to this occasion.
We thank you for this food,
and the kind people who prepared it,
and for the friends with whom we share it.
Most of all,
we thank you for your love
that lives through us
for others.
Amen.*

Main Dishes — 71

Here's a real winner contributed by Donna Sinclair, of North Bay, Ontario. Donna says she got it from her friend Wanda Wallace. Donna is a writer (among many other things) and the author of *Worth Remembering*. When the editors tried this recipe, they felt it was indeed worth remembering. The tasty filling can be made ahead and refrigerated.

Donna Sinclair's
Worth Remembering Tuna Burgers

¼ lb	**processed cheese**, cut in small cubes	125 g
3	**hard-cooked eggs**, chopped	3
7 oz	**tuna**, tin, drained	220 g
2 Tbsp	**green pepper**, chopped	30 mL
3 Tbsp	**onion**, chopped	45 mL
3 Tbsp	**celery**, chopped	45 mL
3 Tbsp	**green pickle relish**	45 mL
3	**olives**, chopped	3
½ cup	**mayonnaise**	125 mL
6	**hamburger buns**	6

Makes 6 servings.

Preheat oven to 450°F.

Mix all ingredients together. Put on buns (open-faced). Cover with foil & bake for 10-15 minutes.

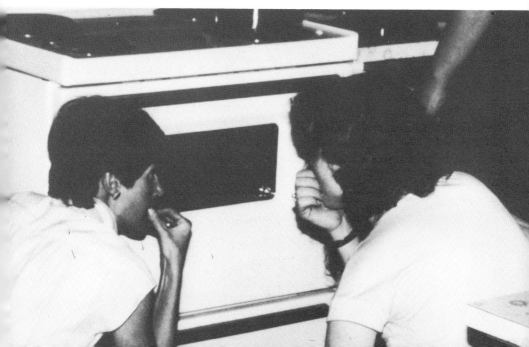

"To be a member of the church, you have to like casseroles," claims Ralph Milton in his book *This United Church of Ours*. If that's the case here's a casserole that makes membership easier. It's easy to prepare and comes from Laura Hawthorn of Bracebridge, Ontario.

Laura Hawthorn's Scallop Casserole

1 lb.	**scallops**, fresh or frozen	450 g
1 tsp	**salt**	5 mL
2 Tbsp	**butter**	30 mL
½ cup	**onion**, minced	125 mL
1½ cups	**celery**, diced	375 mL
1 cup	**mushrooms**, sliced	250 mL
¼ cup	**butter**	60 mL
¼ cup	**flour**	60 mL
1¾ cups	**milk**	430 mL
1 Tbsp	**lemon juice**	15 mL
1 cup	**dry bread crumbs**	250 mL
¼ cup	**cheddar cheese**, grated	60 mL
3 Tbsp	**butter**, melted	45 mL

Makes 6 servings.

Preheat oven to 375°F.

Thaw frozen scallops; spread scallops on a plate, cut large scallops in quarters. Sprinkle with salt & set aside.

Melt 2 Tbsp (30 mL) butter in frying pan. Add onion, celery, & mushrooms & saute over low heat till vegetables are tender.

Meanwhile, melt ¼ cup (60 mL) butter in saucepan. Stir in flour. Gradually add milk, stirring until smooth. Cook until sauce is thickened, stirring constantly. Stir in lemon juice.

Drain liquid from scallops & discard. Add scallops to sauteed vegetables in frying pan. Pour thickened sauce over all. Mix gently & spoon into a shallow 4 cup (1 L) buttered casserole dish.

Combine bread crumbs, grated cheese & 3 Tbsp (45 mL) melted butter. Sprinkle over mixture in casserole.

Bake uncovered at 375°F. 20-30 minutes, or till scallops in the centre of the dish are cooked through.

Whether therefore you eat, or drink, or whatever you do, do it all to the glory of God.

I Corinthians 10; 31

Editing a cookbook can be fun (and fattening) as Anne Nightingale discovered. Having three similar recipes come in, Anne simply took the best elements of each and put them together into this winner. So credit goes to Paula Lock and Bernice Balfour of Vancouver, and Laura Hawthorn of Bracebridge, Ontario.

This dish caused a small riot at radio station CKOV in Kelowna, when talk-show host Terese Elvis invited staff in to taste it. They rated it 9.9 on a scale of 10.

The Bernice, Laura, Paula Salmon Crunch Quiche

PASTRY:

1½ cups	**flour**	375 mL
½ cup	**butter**	125 mL
1 cup	**cheddar cheese**, grated	250 mL
1 tsp	**salt**	5 mL
½ cup	**walnuts**, finely chopped	125 mL

FILLING:

3	**eggs**	3
¾ cup	**sour cream**	180 mL
¼ cup	**mayonnaise**	60 mL
8 oz	**mozzarella** or **swiss cheese**, grated	225 g
½ cup	**onion**, chopped finely	125 mL
7¾ oz	**salmon**, canned	220 g

Makes 8 servings.

Cut flour into butter with pastry blender until crumbly. Stir in cheese, salt & nuts. Reserve ⅔ cup (170 mL) for topping & press remainder onto bottom & sides of a well-greased quiche dish or 10″ (25 cm) pyrex pie plate. (Pie shell can be made ahead & refrigerated until just before filling.)

Preheat oven to 375°F.

Beat eggs in mixing bowl till frothy. Add sour cream, mayonnaise, cheese & onion.

Drain salmon thoroughly, break up with fork & gently stir into egg mixture. Pour into prepared pie shell. Sprinkle reserved crumb topping over quiche.

Bake at 375°F. for 40-45 minutes, or until a knife inserted in the center comes out clean.

A Nova Scotia toast:

> Here's to you, as good as you are,
> And here's to me, as bad as I am;
> As bad as I am, as good as you are,
> I'm as good as you are, bad as I am.

One of Canada's most respected and loved church leaders is Bishop Remi De Roo of the Diocese of Victoria. He shepherds the Roman Catholic faith communities on Vancouver Island and the adjacent Islands, and because of that, often finds himself on or near the sea.

It was no surprise that the good Bishop chose to contribute a tasty seafood recipe with a crunchy texture, one he has enjoyed at one of the many church suppers he's attended.

Bishop De Roo's West Coast Shrimp or Crab Casserole

4 Tbsp	**butter**	60 mL
4 Tbsp	**flour**	60 mL
2 cups	**milk**	500 mL
6	**celery** stalks	6
1	**onion**, large	1
1 cup	**mushrooms**, sliced (optional)	250 mL
2-3½ oz	*****shrimp** or **crab**, tinned	2-113 g
3 cups	**macaroni**, cooked	750 mL
3 cups	**rice**, cooked	750 mL
1½ cups	**green peas**, frozen	375 mL
2 Tbsp	**lemon juice**	30 mL
10 oz	**mushroom soup** or **tomato soup**, can	284 mL
	salt, pepper, garlic powder, to taste	
1 cup	**mozzarella** or **cheddar cheese**, grated	250 mL

Makes 12 servings**.

Preheat oven to 325°F.

In a saucepan, melt butter, blend in flour thoroughly; gradually add milk, stirring until smooth & thickened to make a white sauce.

Chop celery, onion & mushrooms. In a large bowl combine white sauce, chopped vegetables, shrimp, macaroni, rice, peas, lemon juice & soup. Season to taste with salt, pepper & garlic powder.

Transfer to 3 qt. (3 L) casserole. Sprinkle grated cheese on top, cover & bake at 325°F. for 45 minutes, or until bubbling in the centre.

*If you are lucky enough to have access to fresh seafood, by all means use it in place of the canned.

**To serve 6 people, omit the first 3 ingredients (white sauce), use one full can of soup & divide remaining ingredients in half.

Referring to his dislike of fish, Erasmus is quoted as saying, "My heart is Catholic, but my stomach is Lutheran."

Anne Cunningham is pretty busy as Sunday School Superintendent at the Campbell-Stone Church in Calgary. So she appreciates the quickness of this crustless quiche. It's full of protein and nice to serve with a green salad and rolls.

Anne Cunningham's Surprise Pie

7 oz	flaked **tuna, crab, shrimp,** or **ham** flakes, tin	220 g	
1 cup	**sharp cheddar** or **swiss cheese**, grated	250 mL	
2 oz	**cream cheese**, cubed	60 g	
¼ cup	**green onions**, chopped	60 mL	
2 oz	**pimento**, chopped (optional)	60 g	
2 cups	**milk**	500 mL	
4	**eggs**	4	
1 cup	**biscuit mix**	250 mL	
½ tsp	**salt**	2 mL	
dash	**nutmeg**	dash	

Makes 6 servings.

Preheat oven to 375°F.

Combine the fish *or* hamflakes, shredded cheese, creamed cheese, onions & pimento in a greased 10" (25 cm) pie plate.

Beat together the milk, eggs, biscuit mix, salt & nutmeg & pour over the contents of the pie plate.

Bake at 375°F. for 45-50 minutes or until a knife inserted near the center comes out clean. Cool 5 minutes before serving for easier cutting.

Living Message is a national Canadian magazine of the Anglican church, though people of many denominations find it helpful and interesting. Rita Baker is the Editor, and as such, looks for creativity in the material she uses in her magazine and appreciates it in the recipes she uses. Rita also enjoys the creativity of church suppers.

"Each cook puts a little 'self' into the recipe," she says. "A bit of this, a 'smidgen' of that, a few drops of the other. This recipe is like that. It's difficult to be precise about it. Just add or substract whatever you fancy."

Our cookbook editors took Rita at her word and applied a bit of creativity. Rita was quite right of course. You can vary the recipe to suit your personal taste. If you wish, substitute any sea food for the crab, vary the herbs, or use tomato sauce instead of the mushroom soup. And you can serve it either hot or cold. It's nice with salad.

Rita Baker's Sea Shells

1 cup	**macaroni shells**, large	250 mL
1 cup	**bread crumbs**, fine	250 mL
3½ oz	**crabmeat**, can	113 g
¼ cup	**parsley**, fresh	60 mL
¼ tsp	**thyme**, dried	1 mL
1 Tbsp	**dill**, fresh or frozen	15 mL
2 Tbsp	**lemon juice**	30 mL
1	**egg**, beaten	1
1	**green onion**, chopped	1
10 oz	**mushroom soup**, canned	284 mL
½ cup	**milk**	125 mL

Makes 4 servings.

Preheat oven to 350°F.

Cook the shells according to package directions. Drain & rinse with cold water.

Mix breadcrumbs with drained crab; add parsley, thyme, dill, lemon juice & beaten egg. Fill each shell with the crabmeat mixture & place, in a single layer, in a shallow greased casserole dish.

Combine the mushroom soup & milk & spoon over shells. Sprinkle with chopped green onion.

Bake at 350°F. for about 30 minutes.

The man who bites his bread, or eats peas with a knife, I look upon as a lost creature.
W.S. Gilbert

Main Dishes — 77

Dr. Hugh McCullum is the Editor of Canada's "most quoted religious magazine," *The United Church Observer*. Hugh has a fine sense of words and a keen sense of taste, which is why he sent us his favorite fish dish. The lemon flavor blends beautifully with the salmon or trout. And if you're calorie shy, you can make it without the sour cream. It's still fit for the gourmet editor.

Hugh McCullum's Salmon or Trout Steaks with Sour Cream Sauce

6	**fish steaks**-about 1″ (2.5 cm) thick	6
¼ tsp	**salt**	1 mL
1/8 tsp	**pepper**	.5 mL
pinch	**oregano**	pinch
2	**lemons**, thinly sliced	2
¼ cup	**lemon juice**	60 mL
3 Tbsp	**butter**, melted	45 mL
⅓ cup	**green onions**, snipped or:	85 mL
⅓ cup	**Spanish onions**, thinly sliced	85 mL
1 cup	**sour cream**	250 mL
1 tsp	**fresh parsley** chopped	5 mL

Makes 6 servings.

Preheat oven to 450-500°F.

Sprinkle steaks with salt and pepper & pinch of dry oregano. Arrange lemon slices in bottom of greased 9″ x 9″ (22.5 x 22.5 cm) baking dish. Place steaks on top of lemon slices & cover with lemon juice & melted butter.

Sprinkle half of snipped onion on top of steaks & bake in a hot oven, for 25 minutes. Remove from oven, spread sour cream & chopped parsley on steaks & return to oven for 5 minutes.

For serving, garnish with remaining onion & arrange lemon slices from bottom of pan on top of fish steaks.

We are prepared with all our hearts to share our possessions, gold, and all that we have, however little it may be; to sweat and labor to meet the needs of the poor, as the Spirit and the Word of the Lord and true brotherly love teach and imply.

Menno Simons

They probably don't have too many shipwrecks on Okanagan Lake in B.C. where this recipe originates, so it's hard to say how it got the name. But it comes from Gwen Dewhurst who lives in Westbank. This is a family-pleasing, meat-stretching casserole the whole family will enjoy.

Gwen Dewhurst's Shipwreck Casserole

2-3	**onions**, medium	2-3	
5	**potatoes**, sliced	5	
1 tsp	**salt**	5 mL	
½ tsp	**pepper**	2 mL	
½ tsp	**paprika**	2 mL	
1½ lb	**lean ground beef**	675 g	
½ cup	**long grain rice** (uncooked)	125 mL	
1 cup	**celery**, chopped	250 mL	
½ cup	**green pepper**, chopped	125 mL	
½ cup	**mushrooms**, (optional)	125 mL	
10 oz	**tomato soup**, canned	284 mL	
1 cup	**stewed tomatoes** or water	250 mL	

Makes 8-10 servings.

Preheat oven to 350°F.

Lightly butter a 9" x 13" (22.5 x 32.5 cm) pyrex dish.

Slice onions thinly & place in dish. Add sliced potatoes & half the quantities of salt, pepper & paprika. Break up uncooked ground beef & place over potatoes; then shake over remaining salt, pepper & paprika.

Sprinkle over this the rice, celery, green pepper & mushrooms. Lastly combine tomato soup with canned tomatoes or water & pour over casserole, distributing evenly.

Cover dish with tin foil & bake at 350°F. for 2 hours, or till potatoes are cooked.

The liquids may be varied according to taste: use 2 cans tomato soup, or 1 can tomato soup plus 1 cup of beef bouillon. The tin foil keeps the casserole from becoming dry & makes for fluffy rice & thorough blending of flavors.

Taking food and drink is a great enjoyment for healthy people, and those who do not enjoy eating seldom have much capacity for enjoyment or usefulness of any sort.

Charles W. Eliot

Various contributors to this cookbook have claimed to attend "more church suppers than anybody." Betty Lou Clark of Edmonton would certainly be contender for that kind of honor. She manages the United Church Bookstore in Edmonton, and often takes her wares out to conferences and meetings all over Alberta and B.C. And one of the most important things done at all church conferences is eating.

This recipe is inexpensive and is great for taking to potluck suppers. Similar recipes were sent to us by Sue Sewell of Kamloops, B.C., Iris Cornelson of Westbank, B.C., and Susan Butler-Jones of Sault Ste. Marie, Ontario.

Betty Lou Clark's Johnny Mazetti

6 oz	egg noodles	170 g
1 lb.	ground beef	450 g
1 cup	ripe olives, chopped	250 mL
½ cup	celery, chopped	125 mL
1 large	onion, chopped fine	1 large
1	garlic clove, minced or:	1
1 tsp	garlic powder	5 mL
½ cup	water	125 mL
10 oz	tomato soup,	284 mL
2 cups	cheddar cheese, grated, divided	500 mL

Makes 6 servings.

Preheat oven to 375°F.

Cook noodles according to package directions. Do not overcook. Drain & rinse with cold water.

Brown the ground meat. Add olives, celery, onion & garlic & saute until tender. Then add water, tomato soup, 1 cup (250 mL) grated cheese, & drained noodles & gently mix.

Transfer to a greased 2 qt (2 L) casserole, sprinkle with remaining cheese & bake, uncovered, at 375°F. for about 30 minutes or until hot & bubbly.

> One who is full tramples
>   on virgin honey,
>   but to one who is hungry,
>   any bitter thing is sweet.
>   Proverbs 27:7

Enid Dorward remembers the big church suppers they used to have in Oak Lake, Manitoba, in conjunction with the Chataqua. "I remember the infinite variety and number of home-made pies," she says. "Farm ladies make wonderful pies."

Enid is the Resource Centre Librarian at the United Church office in Winnipeg. As such, she finds herself at many potluck suppers and often takes her favorite chili.

Our editors combined her recipe with a similar one received from Iris Cornelson of Westbank, B.C. You can vary the recipe below by including 1½ cups (375 mL) of pumpkin, cubed, and 1 cup (250 mL) of cooked macaroni. If you prefer a milder version of chili, simply reduce the chili powder to about 1 tsp (5 mL).

Enid Dorward's Chili Con Carne

1 lb.	**ground beef**	450 g
1	**onion**, medium, chopped	1
1	**celery** stalk, chopped	1
½	**green pepper**, chopped	½
2-14 oz	**kidney beans**, tins	2-398 mL
10 oz	**tomato soup**	284 mL
7½ oz	**tomato sauce**	220 g
1 Tbsp	**chili powder**	15 mL
2 Tbsp	**brown sugar**	30 mL
	salt & **pepper**, to taste	

Makes 6-8 servings.

Brown meat, onions, celery & pepper together. Add other ingredients & simmer 30 minutes or longer or bake in 350°F. oven for 30 minutes.

For seven days you will eat unleavened bread, and on the seventh day there is to be a feast in honor of God. The rite will serve as a sign on your hand would serve, or a memento on your forehead, and in that way the law of God will be ever on your lips, for God brought you out of Egypt with a mighty hand.

Exodus 13:6, 9-10

These birds are made in turkey factories...
Bob Stewart, a remarkable person and a church historian in Vancouver, B.C., submitted a recipe which he suggested should be taken with a large "pinch of salt."

"We need more ritual in our lives," Bob explains. "We need drama. We need to expand the number of feast days in the Christian year. We need to really do something significant on that oft-ignored Ascension Day.

"So here's my recipe for Ascension Day Turkey. It must be a big, special bird, over 70 pounds. These special birds are made in turkey factories and are hard to find in stores except at Christmas.

"Don't worry about it being too big for the oven, because you cook it outdoors over an open fire. It takes a long time, but good rituals are not to be entered into casually.

"Here's what makes this bird special. You stuff it with lots of spices (use some Biblical spices if you have any) and lots of popcorn. Unpopped popcorn.

"As the turkey begins to cook, all the participants in the ritual should stand in a large circle around the roasting bird, chanting something appropriate. Each person should wear a baseball fielder's glove and running shoes. Hard hats might also be advisable.

"The chanting should build to a climax just as the turkey de-bones itself right before your eyes, in a great greasy pyrotechnical display of meat and mushy popcorn which must be caught as they descend, before they land in the fire and the turkey cremates itself.

"The ritual has great theological import, but this should be explained in a learned paper, not in a cookbook."*

Dr. Stewart is happy to supply copies of his thesis, *The Turkey Explosion in the Canadian Church*, to any who may wish it. Please send a stamped, self-addressed envelope to Dr. Stewart, 6000 Iona Drive, Vancouver, B.C., V6T 1L4.

Cabbage Rolls come from eastern Europe and in many variations. This recipe comes from western Canada, specifically from Olive Dove of Kamloops. It's easy to make. No browning of the meat or pre-cooking of the rice is necessary. Many people say that one of the nicest things about Cabbage Rolls (Holopchi), is that they taste even better when they're re-heated. And they can be frozen for future use.

Olive Dove's Cabbage Rolls

1	**small cabbage**	1
1 lb	**ground beef**	450 g
½ cup	**uncooked rice**	125 mL
¼ tsp	**salt**	1 mL
1/8 tsp	**pepper**	.5 mL
¼ tsp	**garlic powder**	1 mL
1	**onion**, minced	1
4	**bacon** strips, chopped	4
12	**toothpicks**	12
10 oz	**tomato soup**, tin	284 mL
7½ oz	**tomato sauce**, tin	220 mL
1 cup	**water**	250 mL
1 cup	**sour cream**	250 mL

Makes 6 servings.

Preheat oven to 350°F.

In a large saucepan, cover the cabbage with boiling water & boil for 10 minutes to soften leaves. Cut leaves away from core & gently peel from head.

Combine ground beef, uncooked rice, salt, pepper, garlic powder, chopped bacon & onion in a bowl & mix well.

Place about 1 Tbsp (15 mL) of the meat mixture in the center of each leaf & wrap leaf around it as if wrapping a parcel. Hold in place with a toothpick.

Place rolls with open end down in a buttered 1 qt. (1 L) casserole & cover with the tomato soup, sauce & water which have been blended together.

Bake at 350°F. for 1 hour. Add more water during cooking if necessary. Serve with sour cream.

A toast:

May the saddest day of your future,
Be like the happiest day of your past.

Karen and Neale Stead of Oyama, B.C. are both good cooks. The very first recipe tested for this cookbook was checked out in their kitchen.

This delicious, meatless tomato sauce is a winner. It can be served with any pasta.

Karen and Neale Stead's Tomato Cheese Linguine

4 Tbsp	**butter**, divided	60 mL
2	**garlic cloves**, minced	2
14 oz	**canned tomatoes**	398 mL
1 tsp	**basil**	5 mL
	salt & **pepper**, to taste	
1½ Tbsp	**flour**	22 mL
1½ cups	**milk**, hot	375 mL
¼ cup	**parmesan cheese**	60 mL
¾ lb	**linguine**, cooked, drained, buttered	340 g

Makes 6-8 servings

In a saucepan or small skillet, melt 2 Tbsp (30 mL) butter & saute garlic. Add tomatoes, basil, salt & pepper. Simmer while preparing rest of dish.

In another saucepan melt remaining 2 Tbsp (30 mL) butter & stir in flour. Gradually add hot milk & cook & stir until thickened. Add tomato mixture, then stir in parmesan cheese.

Toss with linguine. Serve with more parmesan cheese if desired.

Booths were set up in the horse sheds...
Rev. John and Helen Shearman of the Palermo, Ontario, United Church, remember a grand tradition from the shores of Lake Erie.

"Cheapside and Nanticoke are rural communities on the north shore of the lake. At Cheapside in the early 1900s, a garden party was held each 1st of July with fresh strawberries and ice cream generously served to all present. A program of music, recitations and readings followed.

"In those days, before electrically operated deep freezers, it was a challenge to produce enough ice cream. The Cheapside Ladies Aid solved the problem with great ingenuity: they had it done at the blacksmith's shop.

"The blacksmith owned one of those new gasoline engines. So the freezer was taken over there and hitched to the engine until enough ice cream was made to satisfy the hungry community.

"Sometimes the party was held in the church yard. Booths for serving food and drink were set up in the horsesheds out back, but the church itself was never used for the program afterward. There was simply too much risk that the worldly nature of the songs and recitations might be unsuitable for the hallowed walls of the sanctuary. The community hall was considered a more suitable environment.

If you like lasagne loaded with cheese, you'll really enjoy this recipe which comes from Sheila Storry of Wolfville, Nova Scotia. It's deliciously rich.

Sheila Storry's Wolfville Lasagne

SAUCE:

1 lb.	**ground beef**	450 g
1	**onion**, sliced	1
1 Tbsp	**basil**	15 mL
1 tsp	**Italian herb seasoning**	5 mL
½ tsp	**garlic powder** or:	2 mL
1	**garlic clove**, minced	1
1 tsp	**salt**	5 mL
1 Tbsp	**sugar**	15 mL
28 oz	**canned tomatoes**	796 mL
8 oz	**tomato paste**	225 mL

REMAINING INGREDIENTS:

10 oz	**lasagne noodles**	284 mL
3 cups	**cottage cheese**	750 mL
½ cup	**parmesan cheese**	125 mL
2 Tbsp	**parsley flakes**	30 mL
2	**eggs**, beaten	2
½ tsp	**pepper**	2 mL
1 tsp	**salt**	5 mL
1 lb.	**mozzarella cheese**, sliced	450 g

Makes 8-10 servings.

Preheat oven to 350°F.

In a large skillet, brown the ground beef & onion, drain off fat if necessary. Add herbs, salt & sugar & simmer for 3-4 minutes. Add tomatoes & tomato paste, heat to boiling & simmer sauce, uncovered, for 30 minutes.

Cook the lasagne noodles according to package directions, drain in collander in sink & rinse well with cold water.

Combine cottage cheese, parmesan, parsley flakes, egg, pepper & salt to form a creamy cheese mixture.

Butter a 13" x 9" x 2" (32.5 cm x 22.5 cm x 5 cm) baking dish. Assemble casserole by placing half the noodles in baking dish, then spread with half the cottage cheese mixture, then half the sliced mozzarella, topped with half the sauce. Repeat.

Bake at 350°F. for 45 minutes. Remove from oven & let stand for 20 minutes for easier serving.

"This is an authentic Italian recipe," says Dr. Ted Siverns of St. David's Presbyterian church in Kelowna. "I got it from my wife. She got it from my mother. Mother got it from a friend. The friend's mother was part Italian."

Who could argue with that? Anyway, our editors found that the combination of beef and pork makes a very delicious meat ball. But they were unable to discover why Ted called it "Presbyterian Spaghetti".

Ted Siverns' Presbyterian Spaghetti and Meat Balls

MEAT BALLS:

1 lb	**ground beef**	450 g
1 lb	**ground pork**	450 g
1	**egg**	1
1	**garlic cloves**, crushed	1
1	**bread slice**, broken into small pieces	1
2 Tbsp	**parmesan cheese**	30 mL
1 tsp	**salt**	5 mL
1/8 tsp	**pepper**	.5 mL

Makes about 8 servings.

Mix the meatball ingredients thoroughly & form into balls about 1½" (3.5 cm) in diameter. Brown in a small amount of hot cooking oil.

SAUCE:

2-28 oz	**canned tomatoes**	2-796 mL
5½ oz	**tomato paste**, tin	156 mL
1	**bay leaf**	1
2 Tbsp	**vinegar**	30 mL
2 Tbsp	**sugar**	30 mL
1 tsp	**salt**	5 mL
1/8 tsp	**pepper**	.5 mL
10 oz	**mushrooms**, sliced can	284 mL
1 cup	**celery**, chopped & sauteed (optional)	250 mL
1 cup	**green pepper**, chopped & sauteed (optional)	250 mL

Combine sauce ingredients in a large saucepan. Add browned meatballs & bring to a boil; reduce heat & simmer, uncovered, at least 2 hours.

Serve over spaghetti cooked according to package directions.

Sara's test for cooked spaghetti: Toss a piece of spaghetti against the refrigerator. If it sticks, it's cooked. This method is definitely frowned upon by Elaine Towgood, Sara's mother.

If you own a slow cooker, or are looking for an excuse to get one, consider this recipe from Donna Blois, who has taken this to church suppers at Trinity United in Vernon, B.C. It's meatballs...with a difference.

Donna Blois'
Italian Meatball Stew

MEATBALLS:

1½ lb	**lean ground beef**	675 g
½ cup	**breadcrumbs**, fine	125 mL
2	**eggs**, beaten	2
¼ cup	**milk**	60 mL
2 Tbsp	**parmesan cheese**	30 mL
1 tsp	**salt**	5 mL
1/8 tsp	**garlic salt**	.5 mL
¼ tsp	**pepper**	1 mL
4	**carrots**	4

SAUCE:

6 oz	**tomato paste**, can	175 mL
1 cup	**water**	250 mL
1 cup	**beef bouillon**	250 mL
½ tsp	**oregano**	2 mL
½ tsp	**basil**	2 mL
10 oz pkg	***Italian vegetables**, frozen	280 g

Serves 6.

Combine beef with bread crumbs, eggs, milk, cheese, salt, garlic salt & pepper. Form into golf-ball sized meatballs. Peel carrots & slice into ½" (1 cm) thickness; drop into bottom of slow cooker pot. Arrange meatballs over carrots.

Combine tomato paste with water, bouillon, oregano & basil. Pour over meat. Cover & cook at high about 4 hours. Add partially-thawed vegetables & stir into pot. Continue cooking another half an hour, or till vegetables are tender & sauce thickened.

*As an alternative to buying the frozen veggies, simply steam a combination of about 2 cups (500 mL) of cauliflower, zucchini, onion, green pepper, or your family's preference.

Photo: Bob Greichen

It isn't so much what's on the table that matters, as what's in the chairs.

W.S. Gilbert

"If you've ever tried to cater to one of those low-budget dinners," says M.L. Barmby of Yellow Grass, Saskatchewan, "you can appreciate the problem, when we had to put on a meal for the whole Presbytery. Myrt B. came to our rescue with her tangy meat loaf. Our crew went to work and transformed 30 pounds of hamburger into 'the best-ever meatloaf'.

Apparently the people in Penticton, B.C. know the secret too, because Julie Mezaros of Penticton United Church has prepared a very similar meat loaf for the Men's Club.

One of the nice things about this meatloaf is that it's good cold and slices well for sandwiches.

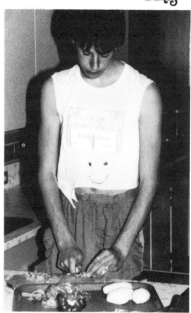

Julie Mezaros' Men's Club Meatloaf

2 cups	**bread crumbs**, soft	500 mL
1½ cups	**milk**	375 mL
1½ lb	**ground beef**	675 g
½ lb	**ground pork**	225 g
2	**eggs**	2
1 large	**onion**, chopped	1 large
1 cup	**celery**, chopped	250 mL
½ tsp	**sage**	2 mL
½ tsp	**paprika**	2 mL
	garlic powder, to taste	
1 tsp	**salt**	5 mL
½ tsp	**pepper**	2 mL
10 oz	**tomato soup**, can	284 mL
1 cup	**tomato juice**	250 mL

Makes 10-12 servings.

Preheat oven to 350°F.

Soak bread crumbs with milk; allow to stand.

Combine ground meats, eggs, onion, celery & spices. Stir in moistened bread crumbs. Press into a large loaf pan (9" x 5" or 22.5 cm x 11 cm).

Bake at 350°F. for 45 minutes. Drain off fat. Combine tomato soup & juice in a small saucepan & pour some over the loaf. Return to oven & continue baking for 45 minutes longer. Let stand 10 minutes before slicing.

Heat any remaining sauce & serve with meatloaf.

With one mind they kept up their daily attendance at the temple, and, breaking bread in private houses, shared their meals with unaffected joy, as they praised God and enjoyed the favor of the whole people.

Acts 2:46

Dr. Gerald Hobbs, who teaches at the Vancouver School of Theology and is currently editing a new hymn book, has lived and worked in eastern France, where he picked up this dish from the people of Alsace. "The name 'Baeckoffe' derives from the practice of earlier generations," says Gerald. They often didn't have their own oven, but would take the dish to their neighboring baker for cooking."

Anne Nightingale who tested this recipe didn't really enjoy the Baeckoffe, but friends whose taste preferences had developed more on continental European lines, found it "good, substantial, and delicious." It reminded Norah Kerr, who is Scottish, of Steak and Kidney Pie. One taster felt it could use a few colorful vegetables like carrots or peas.

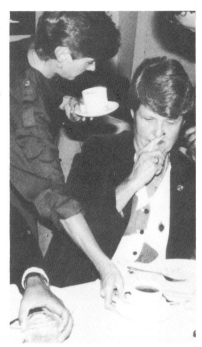

Gerald Hobbs'
Alsatian Baeckoffe

3	**potatoes**, thickly sliced	3
1	**onion**, large	1
2 lb	**beef chuck steaks**	900 g
2	**bay leaf**	2
2	**garlic cloves**, whole	2
	salt & **pepper**, to taste	
	dry white wine & **water** equal parts	
1 cup	**biscuit mix**	250 mL

Makes 6-8 servings.

Preheat oven to 300°F.

"In a commodious oven dish with lid (clay is ideal, but iron or pyrex will serve), place layers of thickly-sliced potato & onion together with slices of assorted meats (inexpensive cuts). Traditionally, they are beef, pork & mutton, but you may vary this according to taste & availability. Season with salt, pepper, bay leaf & garlic cloves. Cover the whole with dry white wine diluted equally with water."

Prepare biscuit mix according to package directions (or make up a small amount of home-made baking powder biscuit dough) & place this around the rim of the dish; cover with the lid & bake at 300°F. for 3-4 hours.

No finer compliment can be paid a cook than to eat freely and with relish of his cooking.
Ralph Conner

The sauce on this dish is really an excellent tomato barbecue sauce and would go well on any meat. The recipe comes to us from Mr. and Mrs. Sherman B. Embree of the West Point Grey Presbyterian Church in Vancouver.

Mr. and Mrs. Embree's
Braised Beef in Barbecue Sauce

1 lb.	**chuck steak**, boneless or:	450 g	
3 lbs	**beef shortribs**	1.35 kg	
1 Tbsp	**vegetable oil**	15 mL	
1	**onion**, chopped	1	
¼ cup	**vinegar**	60 mL	
2 Tbsp	**sugar**	30 mL	
1 cup	**ketchup**	250 mL	
½ cup	**water**	125 mL	
3 Tbsp	**worcestershire sauce**	45 mL	
1 tsp	**prepared mustard**	5 mL	
½ cup	**celery**, sliced	125 mL	
1 tsp	**salt**	5 mL	

Makes 4 servings.
Preheat oven to 350°F.

Brown the steak (whole or cut into chunks) with the onion in hot oil in a heavy skillet.

Add all remaining ingredients. Cover & simmer slowly 1-1½ hours or until tender, or bake in oven at 350°F.

We assume Darryll Brock of Estevan, Saskatchewan doesn't like the messy browning process of most chicken recipes. At least that's one of the nice things about this dish, which also looks good and tastes even better. It's nice served with green vegetables.

Darryll Brock's Orange-Onion Chicken

3½ lbs	**frying chicken**, cut up	1.5 kg	
1 env	**onion soup**, dehydrated	1 env	
6 oz	**orange juice**, frozen concentrate	175 mL	
1 Tbsp	**cornstarch**	15 mL	
½ tsp	**poultry seasoning** or **sage**	2 mL	

Makes 6 servings.

Preheat oven to 350°F.

Place chicken pieces skin side up in a 9" x 13" (22.5 x 32.5 cm) pan. Bake at 350°F. for 15 minutes.

Meanwhile, combine remaining ingredients in saucepan; cook & stir until starch has thickened. Add water if it becomes too thick. Pour sauce over chicken pieces, cover with foil & bake 1 hour.

Uncover, baste with sauce & bake another 15 minutes.

Indian ice cream and salmon...

Those who were there will not soon forget it. A feast for 2,000 people—a feast of barbecued salmon, ooligan (small, smoked fish), moose meat, salmon and herring roe on kelp, "Indian ice cream" made of soapberries, wild rice, and far more. And all of it prepared and served by west coast native people with a sense of fun and efficiency that made it a treat for the soul as well as the palate.

The occasion was the annual meeting of the B.C. Conference of the United Church held in Nanaimo. And the feast celebrated the 100th anniversary of the first powered mission boat to serve the isolated people of Canada's west coast.

Anita Greenaway had a similar experience. "My most memorable church supper was served by the Tsimpshean Indian ladies of Port Simpson United Church, where my husband was minister. They served baked sockeye salmon to a meeting of the Prince Rupert Presbytery, with a style and efficiency that few could match. And for a prairie girl, that salmon was an unbelievable treat!"

We don't know who Noella is, but she hosted a gathering of people from the Thorncliff Catholic Community. "It was a mini-U.N.," says Fr. John M. Lee C.P., of Lloydminster, Alberta. "Noella served this dish because she knew I was on a low fat diet. Everyone enjoyed it."

Fr. Lee, of the Passionist Community of Canada, says this dish is tasty, "and good for low cholesterol diets." Our editors also appreciated the ease of preparation.

If you don't like poultry seasoning, try paprika or dill seed. Even without a seasoning, the chicken will take on a pleasant flavor from the soup.

Fr. John Lee's
Noella's Chicken Dish

2	**frying chicken**, cut up *or* **chicken parts** preferred	2
	poultry seasoning, to taste	
10 oz	**cream of chicken soup**, canned	284 mL
10 oz	**cream of celery soup**, canned	284 mL
10 oz	**cream of mushroom soup**, canned	284 mL

Makes 10-12 servings.

Preheat oven to 350°F.

Remove skin & as much fat as possible from chicken pieces. Rinse in water & pat dry.

Place pieces in two pans to accommodate chicken easily. Sprinkle with poultry seasoning to taste. (Suggest approximately ½ tsp [2 mL] per pan).

Combine contents of soup cans in a mixing bowl & pour evenly over all chicken pieces, ensuring that chicken is covered.

Bake at 350°F., uncovered, for 1 hour.

The pleasure in eating is not in the costly flavor but in yourself.

Horace

Doug Flanders never makes this dish without thinking of the Young Adult Fellowship at Metropolitan United Church in London, Ontario. "Koinonia (A New Testament Greek word meaning 'fellowship') was the name of the group. And what a wonderful fellowship we had there.

"All of us were either working adults or students at the university, and we came together, often over a meal before the evening service, to share love, support, laughter and concerns with one another. It was to such gatherings that I often brought my chicken and rice.

"It tasted good, but what I liked best was what the dish symbolized—the sharing of food in a fellowship of kindness, warmth and love."

Doug, who is Statistic and Information Officer for the United Church, is a young Elder at the Bloor Street United Church.

This is an easy-to-prepare recipe with very rewarding results. If you can't bear deboning chicken breasts, just use cut-up chicken parts. It works almost as well.

Photo: Bob Greichen

Doug Flanders' Koinonia Chicken and Rice

1 cup	**converted rice**	250 mL
1 cup	**water** or **milk**	250 mL
3	**whole chicken breasts**, deboned	3
10 oz	**cream of mushroom soup**, tin	284 mL
10 oz	**water** or **milk**	284 mL
1 env	**dried onion soup mix**	1 env

Makes about 6 servings.

Preheat oven to 350°F.

Place rice on bottom of 2 quart casserole or roasting pan with tight-fitting lid. Add 1 cup (250 mL) water or milk. Cut chicken breasts into small pieces & place on top of rice & liquid.

Cover all with 1 tin of mushroom soup & 1 soup tin full of water or milk. Sprinkle envelope of dried onion soup mix over top.

Bake at 325°F., tightly covered, for 2½ hours & do not open lid.

Serve with a fresh green vegetable.

"This recipe has nothing to do with the religious festival of Passover," says Brian Jackson of Vernon, B.C. "If you don't like spicy food, 'passover' to the next recipe."

Brian enjoyed this recipe at church suppers in India where he served as a missionary. "It's better reheated, so prepare it in the morning or a day ahead, and keep it in the refrigerator. It allows the spices to permeate. Remove any excess fat before reheating it.

This is *real* curried chicken. If you're not used to hot foods, Brian suggests eating it along with a banana to cool your mouth. And he reminds us that in a curry, the liquid is hotter than the solids.

Indian bread (chapattis) goes well with this. Warmed pita bread makes a good substitute. Finish the meal with a few mixed raisins and nuts.

Brian Jackson's
Passover Curried Chicken

2	**frying chickens**, (utility grade is fine)	2
¼ cup	**butter**	60 mL
¼ tsp	**salt**	1 mL
1 tsp	**black pepper**, ground	5 mL
1 Tbsp	**tumeric**	15 mL
¼ tsp	**chili powder**	1 mL
½ tsp	**ground cloves**	2 mL
¾ tsp	**ground cardamom**	4 mL
½ tsp	**ground coriander**	2 mL
1 tsp	**ground ginger**	5 mL
½ tsp	**ground cinnamon**	2 mL
1 tsp	**garlic powder**	5 mL
1 or 2	**hot green peppers**	1 or 2
2 large	**onions**, chopped	2 large
1¼ cups	**chicken stock**	310 mL

Makes 10-12 servings.

Cut up chickens. Boil the backs & necks to make chicken stock.

Heat butter, add all ingredients except chicken pieces, onion & stock. Fry for 5 minutes on medium heat. (This process brings out the flavor of each of the spices.) Add chicken pieces & brown well on all sides. Add chopped onion & cook gently for about 25 minutes, stirring occasionally.

Gradually add stock & simmer, covered, for 1 hour or until chicken is tender.

Serve the curry with steamed rice. Onion & tomato slices make a good garnish. A dish of plain yogurt is also a welcome (and cooling) addition.

There are those who throw chicken wings into the garbage, but cookbook editor Anne Nightingale turns them into a delicious treat. Her recipe is always a treat at church suppers.

Anne also includes a recipe from her late mother-in-law. It's a handy recipe, because the chicken doesn't need browning. And it beats anything "The Colonel" ever cooked.

Anne Nightingale's Barbecued Chicken Wings

3 lbs	chicken wings (or parts)	1.35 g	
¼ cup	ketchup	60 mL	
1½ cups	dry bread crumbs	375 mL	
⅓ cup	honey	85 mL	
1 Tbsp	lemon juice	15 mL	
¼ tsp	garlic powder	1 mL	
¼ tsp	ginger, ground	1 mL	
1 Tbsp	worcestershire sauce	15 mL	
¾ cup	orange or pineapple juice	180 mL	

Makes 6 servings.

Preheat oven to 350°F.

With pastry brush, 'paint' ketchup on chicken pieces, rolling each piece in crumbs after coating.

Bake at 350°F. for 30 minutes on tin foil covered pan, which is large enough to accommodate chicken without crowding.

Combine remaining ingredients in a small saucepan, & heat till honey is melted. Drizzle sauce over partially-cooked chicken. Loosely cover with tin foil, & continue baking for 15 minutes. Remove foil and bake for final 15 minutes.

Oma Nightingale's Crispy Fried Chicken

1	chicken, (fryer, cut up or parts)	1	
½ cup	butter	125 mL	
½ tsp	dry mustard	2 mL	
1½ tsp	paprika	7 mL	
1 tsp	salt	5 mL	
1/8 tsp	pepper	.5 mL	
1½ cups	dry bread crumbs	375 mL	

Makes 6 servings.

Preheat oven to 350°F.

Wash chicken pieces & pat dry.

In small saucepan, over low heat, melt butter & add mustard, paprika, salt & pepper.

Dip chicken pieces in spiced butter & roll in bread crumbs. Place on a cookie sheet which has been covered with lightly oiled tin foil.

Bake, uncovered, at 350°F. for 1 hour.

Main Dishes — 95

Chicken Cordon Bleu sounds pretty exotic, and perhaps doesn't belong in a book of "easy to prepare" recipes. But our testers discovered that this recipe wasn't really that hard to do or that expensive. It came from Orma Kyle of West Point Grey Presbyterian Church in Vancouver. She's part of the Margaret Creelman Missionary Group.

This may not be usual fare at pot-luck suppers, but you are certain to get comments if you bring it. And Ralph Milton remembers a dinner at St. Paul's United in Estevan, Saskatchewan, catered by the Men's Group. Several hundred people dined in style on Chicken Cordon Bleu.

Orma Kyle's Chicken Cordon Bleu

3 whole	**chicken breasts**, de-boned	3 whole	
6	thin slices **cooked ham**	6	
6	**swiss cheese**, slices	6	
⅓ cup	**flour** to coat chicken rolls	85 mL	
¼ cup	**oil**	60 mL	
½ cup	**water**	125 mL	
1 tsp	**chicken flavor gravy base**	5 mL	
½ lb	**fresh mushrooms** or:	225 g	
10 oz	**mushrooms,** sliced canned	284 mL	
½ cup	**sauterne wine**	125 mL	
2 Tbsp	**flour**	30 mL	
¼ cup	**water**	60 mL	

Makes 6 servings.

Preheat oven to 350°F.

Cut de-boned chicken breasts in half lengthwise. Pound or press them as flat as possible. With chicken skin side down, place ham slice on top of each, then cheese. Roll up like a jelly roll, folding in loose ends. Tie with string (which can be snipped & removed just before serving).

Coat rolls with flour & brown in hot oil. Remove from pan & place in a 9" x 9" (22.5 x 22.5 cm) baking dish. In pan, combine ½ cup (125 mL) water, gravy base, mushrooms & wine. Heat, stirring to remove crusty chicken pieces. Pour broth over chicken in dish. Cover, bake at 350°F. for 1 hour or until tender.

Transfer chicken to platter. Remove strings. Blend flour & ¼ cup (60 mL) cold water. Add to gravy in pan & stir until thick. Pour some over chicken & pass remaining gravy.

When the small Hungarian community in Kelowna, B.C. meets for worship, they usually have a meal together too. Irene Szakal often prepares Chicken Paprikas for these events. She sent us this recipe, but then so did another Hungarian from Willowdale, Ontario. Maria Booth also remembers her roots, and wanted this recipe included.

Maria suggests that this recipe will feed a crowd with the addition of cooked rice to the gravy. Other meats such as beef or pork can be sustituted for the chicken in the paprikas.

Maria and Irene's Chicken Paprikas with Sour Cream and Dumplings

CHICKEN:

2 Tbsp	**oil**	30 mL
3-4 lbs	**frying chicken**, cut up	1½-2 kg
1 large	**onion**, chopped	1 large
1	**green pepper**, diced	1
2 Tbsp	**paprika**	30 mL
¼ tsp	**black pepper**	1 mL
1 tsp	**salt**	5 mL
1½ cups	**water**	375 mL
14 oz	**canned tomatoes**, broken (optional)	398 mL
1	**garlic clove**, minced (optional)	1
1¼ cups	**sour cream**	310 mL

IRENE'S DUMPLINGS:

2	**eggs**	2
½ cup	**water**	125 mL
½ tsp	**salt**	2 mL
1⅓ cups	**flour**	335 mL

Makes 6 servings.

In a Dutch oven brown chicken lightly in hot oil for 10 minutes. Remove chicken pieces & saute onions & green pepper. Add seasonings, then water, tomatoes & garlic & stir. Add browned chicken pieces, cover & let simmer slowly just until tender—about 45 minutes.

When cooked, set aside chicken pieces & add sour cream to the liquid & mix well. (If necessary, thicken gravy with flour.) Transfer cooked dumplings to Dutch oven & arrange chicken on top. Heat thoroughly & serve.

Beat eggs, add water & salt. Stir in flour. Drop by teaspoonfuls into boiling salted water & cook about 10 minutes or until dumplings float to the surface; drain & add to Paprikas.

Who satisfies thy mouth with good things; so that thy youth is renewed like an eagle's.
Psalm 103;5

Marjorie Smith is the organist at the Conway United Church in Ellerslie, Prince Edward Island. She enjoys making this casserole for suppers at her church. Jean Swann of Westbank, B.C. had a very similar recipe which she kindly sent to us.

The celery and onion give a nice crunchy texture to this dish. If you prefer a mild onion flavor, you might want to saute the onions in a small amount of butter before you mix them with the other ingredients.

Marjorie Smith's Chicken Casserole

2 cups	**cooked chicken** or **turkey**, cubed	500 mL	
1½ cups	**macaroni** or **rice**, cooked	375 mL	
1 cup	**onion**, chopped	250 mL	
1 cup	**celery**, chopped	250 mL	
10 oz	**cream of chicken soup**, can	284 mL	
½ cup	**mayonnaise**	125 mL	
3	**eggs**, hard-cooked & sliced	3	
½ cup	**dry breadcrumbs**	125 mL	
1 Tbsp	**butter**, melted	15 mL	

Makes 6 servings.

Preheat oven to 350°F.

Combine chicken, macaroni, onion & celery. Blend cream of chicken soup & mayonnaise together then add to chicken & mix well. Gently fold in sliced eggs & spoon into a 2 qt (2 L) casserole.

Combine crumbs & melted butter. Sprinkle over chicken mixture. Bake at 350°F. for 45 minutes (microwave for 11 minutes).

Thanking God for our freedom...

It is always hard to "sing the Lord's song in a strange land." But people do, and often with a passion and conviction that those of us who have never really known persecution find hard to understand.

Irene (Kovack) Szakal of Kelowna, sings in the choir at First United Church, but she also worships with her own Hungarian community. "Most of our people faced tragedy (or impending tragedy) back home and fled for their lives," she says. "But God lived on in these immigrants (as in most of those left behind), and we worship together here in Kelowna using local churches and inviting Hungarian ministers from other cities. No matter what our denomination, we worship as one, thanking God for this our adopted home and for our freedom.

"Then after the service we have a program, and of course a supper. And we serve chicken paprikas!"

Church suppers happen all over the world. Rev. Beverley Milton of Winfield, B.C. discovered this recipe at a church supper in the Philippines where she served as a missionary.
This is delicious served over hot rice.

Photo: Lloyd Milton

Beverley Milton's Pork Adobo

½ cup	**vinegar**	125 mL
¼ cup	**soy sauce**	60 mL
2	**garlic cloves**, minced	2
¼ tsp	**black pepper**	1 mL
½	**bay leaf**	½
	salt, to taste	
2 lbs	**pork shoulder**	900 g
2 Tbsp	**vegetable oil**	30 mL

Makes 6 servings.

Combine vinegar, soy sauce, garlic, pepper, bay leaf & salt in a bowl to make marinade. Cube or slice pork into small pieces & soak in marinade for ½ hour.

Drain meat, reserving marinade. Saute meat in hot vegetable oil. Add marinade & simmer for 5 minutes.

Christmas in a far country...

Brian Jackson of Vernon, B.C., a former missionary in India, remembers a very different, but equally marvelous church supper.

"In the village of Rasalpura in Central India, the congregation of Smillie Memorial Chapel decided to have a Christmas dinner. Early in Advent the fund-raising began. It was a big undertaking, because they wanted to be sure there'd be enough food for all.

"A cook was hired. He came and prepared a fireplace on which he cooked a great cauldron of goat meat curry and another of equal size filled with rice (pilau). The cooking began 24 hours in advance, with members of the church taking turns in assisting the cook in the all-night all-day vigil.

"The excitement was great when mealtime arrived! About two hundred people gathered to share this special feast, which was served on disposable plates made of leaves, which somehow managed to hold the liquid curry. We were seated on the ground so maybe we didn't know how much seepage there really was.

"When perspiration trickled down our faces, and plugged sinuses suddenly came clear, we knew we had *hot* curry.

"It was a wonderful way to celebrate Christmas in a far country, with a meal fit for a King!"

Author Ralph Milton (*Through Rose-Colored Bifocals*) remembers a particular church supper in the tiny basement of the East Trail United Church, where this recipe originates.

"We had eaten just far too much, and we were feeling very content and very happy. The after-dinner speaker—I don't remember his name—soon had us almost falling off our chairs with laughter. He seemed to pile one joke on top of another until our sides ached.

"Then just as the laughter peaked, he said some words that I'll never forget. 'If you know how to laugh; you know how to pray. Let us pray.' "

We don't know if Marg and Doug MacArthur were at that dinner, but if they were, they probably brought these pork chops.

Our testers discovered that they stay nicely moist in the sauce; and are great served with fluffy rice and a green salad.

Ed Read of Westbank sent us a very similar sauce recipe which he uses on spareribs. Boil the spareribs for one hour, drain and place them in a roaster, then treat them as the recipe indicates for pork chops.

Marg and Doug MacArthur's Pineapple Pork Chops

6-8	**pork chops**	6-8
1 Tbsp	**oil**	15 mL
14 oz	**pineapple chunks**, canned	398 mL
1 cup	**brown sugar***	250 mL
2 Tbsp	**soy sauce**	30 mL
¼ cup	**vinegar**	60 mL
1 cup	**water**	250 mL
2 Tbsp	**soy sauce**	30 mL
2 Tbsp	**cold water**	30 mL
2 Tbsp	**corn starch**	30 mL

In frying pan over medium heat, brown pork chops in oil. Place in roaster.

Combine pineapple chunks & juice, brown sugar (*may be reduced to ½ cup - 125 mL), 2 Tbsp (30 mL) soy sauce, vinegar & 1 cup (250 mL) water. Pour over pork chops & bake, covered, at 350°F. for 1 hour.

Before serving combine 2 Tbsp. (30 mL) soy sauce, 2 Tbsp (30 mL) water & cornstarch & stir into sauce in roaster. Heat on stove top till thickened, stirring constantly.

Whenever there's a dish of devilled eggs at a pot-luck supper, it disappears almost immediately. That's why Pat McCoubrey of the Winfield United Church enjoys bringing this very different recipe. It's a delicious variation on an old favorite, and makes a nice large dish for a group.

Pat McCoubrey's Hot Devilled Eggs

10	**eggs**	10
⅓ cup	**mayonnaise**	85 mL
¼ tsp	**dry mustard**	1 mL

Makes 10 servings.

Hard cook eggs & cool thoroughly. Shell eggs, cut in halves & scoop out yolks into a mixing bowl. Break yolks up with fork; add mayonnaise & dry mustard, stirring until creamy. Spoon yolk mixture back into halved whites & place in a large shallow dish, in a single layer.

SAUCE:
½ lb	**mushrooms**, fresh	225 g
2 Tbsp	**butter**	30 mL
3 Tbsp	**flour**	45 mL
½-10 oz	**mushroom soup**, can	½-284 mL
1 cup	**light cream**	250 mL
1 cup	**cheddar cheese**, grated	250 mL
½ tsp	**curry powder**	2 mL
1 tsp	**worcestershire sauce**	5 mL

Saute cleaned & sliced mushrooms in a lightly-oiled frying pan. Drain off any liquids.

Melt butter in medium saucepan, add flour stirring well. Add soup, cream & mushrooms. Add cheese & heat through until cheese melts. Add curry powder & worcestershire sauce & pour over eggs in dish.

TOPPING:
½ cup	**soft breadcrumbs**	125 mL
1 Tbsp	**butter**, melted	15 mL
1/8 tsp	**onion salt**	.5 mL
1 Tbsp	**parsley**, chopped	15 mL

Combine topping ingredients & sprinkle around sides of dish. Serve at once.

> All human history attests
> That happiness for man—the hungry sinner—
> Since Eve ate apples, much depends on dinner.
> — Byron

From Wyman Memorial United Church in Hudson, Quebec, comes a recipe for Scotch Eggs. At first glance, this recipe contributed by Mrs. Howell Evans, may appear "fussy" to prepare. But the ingredients actually go together quickly, and they are delicious with the tomato sauce.

If you wish, you can serve them cold, cut in quarters, as an appetizer.

Mrs. Howell Evans' Scotch Eggs

1 lb	**lean ground beef**	450 g
14 oz	**tomato sauce**, canned, divided	398 mL
6	**anchovy fillets**, finely chopped	6
dash	**pepper**	dash
8	**eggs**, hard-cooked	8
2	**eggs**, raw	2
2 cups	**dry bread crumbs**, fine	500 mL
1 tsp	**lemon juice**	5 mL

Combine ground beef, ¼ cup (60 mL) of tomato sauce, anchovies & pepper. Divide into 8 equal parts.

Peel hard-cooked eggs & wrap each with a portion of meat mixture.

Break raw eggs into bowl & beat lightly with a fork. Dip meat-covered eggs in beaten eggs & then roll in bread crumbs.

Deep fry eggs, two at a time, in hot fat (375°F.) till browned & crisp *or* pan-fry eggs in a little oil, turning to cook all sides evenly.

Heat remaining tomato sauce with lemon juice. Cut eggs in halves & spoon sauce over.

Photo: Berkeley Studio

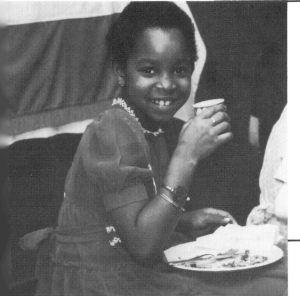

Long before the ecumenical movement...

Sister Katherine McCaffrey of Ottawa says the ecumenical movement may have started over church suppers. Sister Katherine, who is the Assistant General Secretary of the Canadian Religious Conference, says "as a child, long before the ecumenical movement, my most pleasant and positive memories of Christians of other faiths came from attending their church suppers."

Bonnie Brennan has a delightful, sometimes "slightly crazy" job at the Canadian Conference of Catholic Bishops office in Ottawa. As such, she gets to know and work with every Bishop and Archbishop and Cardinal in Canada.

Bonnie didn't send a recipe, but she had a few suggestions. "It would be fun to make it a people book," she said, "rather than just a cookbook." Which is exactly what we've tried to do.

Bonnie also asked for a good macaroni and cheese recipe, which she remembers as a traditional Friday dish in her Catholic home in the days when Fridays were meatless.

Church suppers usually have a great variety of this kind of casserole, so here in Bonnie's honor, is the very best one our editors could find in their extensive files.

Bonnie Brennan's Macaroni and Cheese with Tomato

1½ cups	**elbow macaroni**, uncooked	375 mL
½ cup	**milk**	125 mL
2 Tbsp	**onion**, chopped	30 mL
1 Tbsp	**parsley**, dried	15 mL
1½ cups	**cheddar cheese**, grated	375 mL
	salt & pepper, to taste	
1 cup	**canned tomatoes**	250 mL

Makes 4 servings.

Preheat oven to 350°F.

Cook macaroni until tender, according to package directions. Remove from heat, drain in collander & rinse with cold water. Return to saucepan.

Add remaining ingredients, breaking up tomatoes with fork. Heat over medium till cheese begins to melt.

Pour mixture into a buttered 4 cup (1 L) casserole dish & bake, uncovered, at 350°F. for 30 minutes. Serve hot.

Before baking, you may wish to top casserole with cracker crumbs or buttered bread crumbs for a crunchy topping.

Very Good

Many people never try a souffle because they're afraid it'll fall when it cools. That doesn't seem to happen with this recipe from Jessie Mawhinney of Kelowna, B.C. It's firm and fluffy and is a great idea for lunch.

Jessie Mawhinney's Cheese Souffle

1 cup	**milk**, divided	250 mL
1 cup	**soft white bread crumbs**	250 mL
3 Tbsp	**butter**	45 mL
3 Tbsp	**flour**	45 mL
½ tsp	**salt**	2 mL
dash	**cayenne**	dash
1 cup	**sharp cheddar cheese**, grated	250 mL
3	**egg yolks**, beaten	3
3	**egg whites**	3

Makes 6 servings.

Preheat oven to 350°F.

Pour ½ cup (125 mL) milk over bread crumbs & let stand.

Melt butter in saucepan, blend in flour, salt & cayenne. Add ½ cup (125 mL) milk, stirring until smooth. Cook over low heat till thickened, stirring constantly. Add cheese & stir till smooth. Remove from heat. Add soaked bread crumbs & beaten egg yolks. Cool.

Beat egg whites in glass bowl till stiff. Fold in egg yolk mixture.

Pour into buttered 4 cup (1 L) souffle dish or small casserole. Place dish in pan of warm water.

Bake at 350°F. about 50 minutes, or till knife inserted in center comes out clean.

My first experience of Christian sharing...

For many people, church suppers or picnics have been the first introduction to the support and fellowship people find in their church. Connie Bickford of Burnaby, B.C., tells of just such an experience.

"When I was very new to this congregation, a very timid and shy mother, I took my sons to one of the church family picnics. There was a family who didn't know me at all, but they shared their large pot of chili with us and with others.

"That was my first experience of Christian sharing."

Elaine and John Towgood run an apple orchard overlooking beautiful Wood Lake in B.C.'s Okanagan Valley. They often get large groups of visitors in the sunny Okanagan summertime, and Elaine, one of the editors of this book, likes to get things like "brunch" prepared ahead of time. That's why she selected this delightful recipe.

Elaine Towgood's Baked Brunch Souffle

4 cups	**day-old bread,** cubed (brown or white)	1 L
2 cups	**cheddar cheese,** grated	500 mL
10	**eggs,** slightly beaten	10
4 cups	**milk**	1 L
1 tsp	**dry mustard**	5 mL
1 tsp	**salt**	5 mL
¼ tsp	**onion powder**	1 mL
dash	**pepper**	dash
½ lb	**bacon**	225 g
½ cup	**mushrooms,** sliced	125 mL

Makes 12 servings.

Arrange bread cubes in a greased 9" x 13" (22.5 x 32.5 cm) baking dish. Sprinkle with cheese. Beat together eggs, milk, mustard, salt, onion powder & pepper. Pour evenly over cheese & bread.

Cover & refrigerate overnight.

Preheat oven to 325°F.

Fry bacon till crisp; drain on paper towel & crumble when cool. Saute sliced mushrooms in bacon fat till golden. Sprinkle over bread cubes along with crumbled bacon.

Bake uncovered at 325°F. for 1 hour, or until set. Check for doneness by inserting a knife in center.

Here's something from the sunny Greek islands. It's pronounced Spana-kop′-it-a. Pat Johnson who does outreach work for the Kamloops United Church sent it to us.

It's a delicious meatless dish that's loaded with protein...and calories! But it's worth every bite.

By the way, filo pastry can usually be found in a package in the frozen food section of your supermarket. The 'how-to work with' instructions on the package are often very helpful.

Pat Johnson's Spanakopeta (Spinach Pie)

3-10 oz	**frozen spinach**, pkg thawed & drained	3-310 mL
½ cup	**parsley**, chopped	125 mL
½ cup	**fresh dill**, chopped or:	125 mL
2 Tbsp	**dried dill**	30 mL
2 cups	**green onions**, chopped	500 mL
1 tsp	**salt**	5 mL
2 Tbsp	**olive oil** (or cooking oil)	30 mL
3 cups	**onions**, chopped	750 mL
¼ tsp	**pepper**	1 mL
½ lb	**feta cheese**, crumbled	225 g
½ lb	**farmers** or **cheddar cheese**, shredded	225 g
3	**eggs**	3
¾ cup	**butter**	180 mL
12	**filo pastry leaves**	12

Makes about 16 servings.

Preheat oven to 375ºF.

Combine spinach, parsley, dill, green onions & salt in bowl. Let stand 10 minutes, then press out liquid.

Heat oil in a large skillet, saute the chopped onion. Add the spinach mixture with the pepper & cheeses. Beat the eggs & mix into the spinach/onion mixture. Mix well.

Brush a 9" x 13" (22.5 x 32.5 cm) baking dish with melted butter, then place 6 layers of filo pastry on bottom, brushing each layer with melted butter. Spread filling evenly on top, then cover with remaining filo pastry, brushing each layer with the melted butter. Be sure to butter the top layer well.

With a sharp knife, score the top layer into squares. Bake in a 375ºF. oven for 30 minutes or until golden brown. Serve warm.

The Lord God says this: The fast of the fourth month, the fast of the fifth, the fast of the seventh and the fast of the tenth are to become gladness and happiness and days of joyful feasting for the House of Judah. But love the truth and peace!

Zechariah 8:18-19

There's something very basic and fundamentally delicious about beans. Maybe that's why we received so many recipes for beans. The one below comes from Iris Cornelson of Westbank, B.C., but there was another from Pat Litke of Calgary for "Stampede Beans" which contains no meat, but includes a tin of kidney beans. And Marjorie Hannah of Kelowna, B.C. makes a bean dish including the hamburger and the canned pork and beans, without pineapple.

Ilene Patterson of Winfield, B.C., is the editor of the Anglican Diocesan paper, *High-way*. Hers is a slow cooker recipe for busy people.

Iris Cornelson's Hula Hula Beans

1 lb	**ground beef**	450 g	
28 oz	**dark brown pork & beans**, canned	796 mL	
15 oz	**pineapple chunks** canned	426 mL	
2 Tbsp	**brown sugar**	30 mL	
¼ tsp	**ginger**	1 mL	
2 tsp	**soy sauce**	10 mL	
1/8 tsp	**pepper**	.5 mL	
1 Tbsp	**prepared mustard**	15 mL	
2 shakes!	**ketchup**	2 shakes!	

Makes 6 servings.

Preheat oven to 350°F.

Brown the ground beef, add remaining ingredients & mix well. Pour into casserole dish & bake at 350°F. for 20-30 minutes.

Ilene Patterson's Baked Beans

2 cups	**dried beans**, red or white	500 mL	
5 cups	**water**	1.25 L	
1	**onion**, chopped finely	1	
1 tsp	**salt**	5 mL	
¼ lb	**bacon** or **pork**	112 g	
¼ cup	**molasses**	60 mL	
2 Tbsp	**brown sugar**	30 mL	
1 tsp	**dry mustard**	5 mL	
¼ cup	**ketchup**	60 mL	

Wash & sort beans. Put beans, water, onion, salt & bacon in slow cooker & cook on low overnight, or approx. 10 hours. In the morning drain beans, reserving liquid. Transfer beans to oven-proof dish.

Combine molasses, brown sugar, dry mustard, ketchup & 1 cup of bean liquid— add to cooked beans, stirring well.

Cook, covered, in 300°F. oven for approx. 2 hours longer, stirring occasionally & adding more liquid if necessary.

A highlight of the year for Barbara Klich is the annual Mass and reception put on by the Spiritans, a group of priests who used to be known as the Holy Ghost Fathers. They work in Africa in areas of greatest need. "We knew about the Ethiopian crisis long before the media told us about it," says Barbara.

Barbara enjoys the gathering of "old and new friends who come together to renew acquaintances over the best sandwiches and coffee and little cakes." So she suggested we include a "fancy sandwich loaf recipe". Elaine and Anne sorted through many possibilities before settling on this one, a "three-in-one" creation you might want to make for a special occasion.

Barbara Klich's' Fancy Sandwich Loaf

1	**brown bread** sandwich loaf	1
FILLINGS		
SEAFOOD:		
7½ oz	**salmon** (or any seafood), canned	220 g
3 Tbsp	**mayonnaise**	45 mL
1 tsp	**lemon juice**	5 mL
EGG SALAD:		
6	**eggs**, hard-cooked	6
2	**green onions**, chopped	2
3 Tbsp	**mayonnaise** salt & **pepper**, to taste	45 mL
HAM AND CUCUMBER:		
1	**English cucumber**, sliced thinly	1
¼ lb	**lean ham**, thinly sliced	112 g
1 lb	**cream cheese**, softened	450 g
½ cup	**light cream**	125 mL
¼ cup	**butter**, softened **parsley**, garnish	60 mL

Makes about 40 half-slices.

Have the bakery remove crusts from bread & slice lengthwise into 4 long pieces. Butter one side of three pieces & lay these out on working surface.

Drain salmon & break up with a fork. Combine remaining ingredients for seafood filling & spread this mixture on one long piece of bread. Cover this with a buttered piece of bread, buttered side up.

Shell eggs, break up with a fork & add onion & mayonnaise. Mix well & spread on second layer of bread. Top with another slice.

Arrange slices of ham over length of third layer & place cucumbers on top. Finally, lay the unbuttered bread on top.

Whip softened cream cheese, gradually adding light cream till of a "frosting" consistency. Frost sides & top of sandwich loaf. Garnish with parsley & refrigerate till serving time. When loaf is sliced, the cross section will show the three fillings!

St. Augustine's Anglican Church in Saltcoats, Saskatchewan has an annual pancake supper on Shrove Tuesday. The chief pancake maker in Saltcoats is Tom Neal, who is also on call to make pancakes for two or three other big community events each year.

Tom's recipe for pancakes was designed to serve 60, which is a bit larger than the average family using this book.

Another recipe came from the "Fellowship Team" at Campbell-Stone Church in Calgary. They called them "Panacons" and were specifically designed for Calgary's famous Stampede week. The main feature of this cowboy recipe was a handful of crisp, crumbled bacon tossed into the batter.

The recipe below comes from Bonnie Green, who heads the Human Rights and Justice office for the United Church of Canada. There's a story behind this recipe and its title.

"In our family, my husband makes the breakfast and lunch. Having been brought up to fear attacks of scurvy and beri-beri if he serves cold cereal, he has become quite an excellent cook, provided you catch him before noon.

"His pancakes are so famous, they've found their way into the Men's Club's pancake breakfasts. To me, they're "liberation pancakes" because they're the backbone of one church meal where the women don't have to do the cooking!"

You can make these pancakes special by adding blueberries to the batter, or a hot fruit sauce when serving. Actually, it's amazing what you can add to pancake batter. If you have kids around, you can invite them to help you experiment. You'll have some most "interesting" variations.

Bonnie Green's
Liberation Pancakes

2 cups	**flour**	500 mL	Makes about 24 pancakes
2 Tbsp	**sugar**	30 mL	Mix together flour, sugar, baking powder, & salt in large mixing bowl.
4 tsp	**baking powder**	20 mL	
1 tsp	**salt**	5 mL	
2	**eggs**	2	In small bowl beat eggs lightly; add melted butter or oil, milk & buttermilk. Stir together.
¼ cup	**butter** or **oil**	60 mL	
1½ cups	**milk**	375 mL	Make a "well" in the center of the dry ingredients & pour in egg mixture. Stir until *just* combined.
¾ cup	**buttermilk**	180 mL	

Cook on lightly greased frying pan till bubbles form. Flip & cook on other side till golden.

A delightful way to share...

Please send _____ copies (at 12^{95}, plus $1 shipping, each) of

Those Marvelous Church Suppers

to:
Name: _____

Address: _____

City or Town: _____ Prov: _____ Postal Code: _____

My cheque or money order for _____ is enclosed.

Mail to:
Wood Lake Books, Inc.   or Those Marvelous Church Suppers
Box 700   Box 8066, Station F,
Winfield, BC,   Edmonton, AB,
V0H 2C0   T6H 4N9

A delightful way to share...

Please send _____ copies (at 12^{95}, plus $1 shipping, each) of

Those Marvelous Church Suppers

to:
Name: _____

Address: _____

City or Town: _____ Prov: _____ Postal Code: _____

My cheque or money order for _____ is enclosed.

Mail to:
Wood Lake Books, Inc.   or Those Marvelous Church Suppers
Box 700   Box 8066, Station F,
Winfield, BC,   Edmonton, AB,
V0H 2C0   T6H 4N9

A grace...

*Great God, giver of life,
we gather to share this meal
and this fellowship.
We are thankful for this nourishing food;
we are thankful for these loving people.
Help us to share ourselves
with each other
just as we share this food.
Help us to be with each other
in love and honesty,
and to speak your purpose for humankind
in all that we say
in all that we are.
Amen.*

This cheesecake recipe was used in Rockyford, Alberta at one of their annual dinner-theatre events. June Churchill and Ida Lauridsen of the Rockyford United Church say their group of 50 active church members hosted the event for their community of 400.

"We invited the amateur theatre group from a neighboring community to put on the play. We provided the dinner and elaborate table decorations. Each year, we've been sold out in advance. It's a great way to introduce theatre to rural communities."

This is cheesecake with a delicious difference. It's an easy and an impressive dessert.

June and Ida's Bavarian Apple Torte

BASE:
½ cup	**butter**	125 mL
⅓ cup	**sugar** (may be reduced)	85 mL
¼ tsp	**vanilla**	1 mL
1 cup	**flour**	250 mL

FILLING:
8 oz	**cream cheese**, pkg	225 g
¼ cup	**sugar**	60 mL
1	**egg**, beaten	1
1 tsp	**vanilla**	5 mL

TOPPING:
4	**apples**, sliced	4
⅓ cup	**sugar**	85 mL
½ tsp	**cinnamon**	2 mL
¼ cup	**almonds**, slivered	60 mL

Makes 12 servings.

Preheat oven to 450°F.

Cream together butter, sugar & vanilla; add flour & blend well. Cover the bottom & 1" (2.5 cm) up the sides of a 9" (22.5 cm) spring form pan.

Have cream cheese at room temperature & blend together with sugar, using electric mixer. Add beaten egg & vanilla & mix well. Pour over base.

Toss together apples, sugar, cinnamon & almonds. Spoon over cheese mixture.

Bake at 450°F. for 10 minutes; then at 400°F. for 25 minutes.

The tradition started when the power went off...

It's wonderful how church supper traditions get started. Some of the nicest traditions just happen.

At the United Church in Forest, Ontario, they have a tradition of coal oil lamps, which lend a cozy, warm atmosphere to the church basement. According to Rev. Bill Steadman, the tradition started a few years ago when the power went off. Somebody remembered the old lamps, brought them out, and it became a grand tradition.

This dessert is so sinfully rich, you probably wouldn't dare take it near a church. It's probably best served to a small group of decadent friends at home on a winter evening with the drapes drawn. Then you can utter a short prayer of confession when you stand on the bathroom scales the next morning.

Berna Hull of Donway United Church in Don Mills, Ontario, calls this a "musician's special" though she doesn't say why. We suspect that even a person with a totally tin ear would enjoy it just as much.

Berna Hull's Quadraphonic Delight

BASE:
1 cup	**flour**	250 mL
½ cup	**butter**	125 mL
1 cup	**pecans** or **walnuts**, chopped	250 mL

TOPPING:
2 cups	**frozen whipped topping**, divided	500 mL
1 cup	**icing sugar**	250 mL
8 oz	**cream cheese**, softened	225 g
4 oz	**vanilla instant pudding**, pkg.	113 g
4 oz	**chocolate instant pudding**, pkg.	113 g
3 cups	**milk**	750 mL

Makes 12 servings.

Preheat oven to 325°F.

Combine flour, butter & nuts & press into a buttered 9" x 13" (22.5 x 32.5 cm) pan. Bake at 325°F. for 20 minutes. Cool on rack.

Meanwhile, mix 1 cup (250 mL) of the whipped topping with the icing sugar & softened cream cheese. Spread carefully on cooled crust.

Combine instant puddings & 3 cups (750 mL) milk according to package directions & spread on cheese mixture. Top with remaining dessert topping.

Chill 2-3 hours or overnight.

Note - to make in a 9" (22.5 cm) square pan, repeat the base, but use half the other ingredients.

Let the stoics say what they please. We do not eat for the good of living, but because the meat is savory and the appetite is keen.

Emerson

There are purists who claim a cheesecake must be the result of long and difficult effort in order to be tasty. Sue Sewell of Kamloops isn't one of those people. She offers this quick and easy dessert which scores points in both taste and appearance.

Sue Sewell's No-Bake Cheesecake Dessert

BASE:
1½ cups	**graham wafer** crumbs	375 mL	
¼ cup	**butter**, melted	60 mL	
¼ cup	**sugar**	60 mL	

FILLING:
4 oz	**cream cheese**, softened	113 g	
½ cup	**icing sugar**	125 mL	
½ tsp	**vanilla**	2 mL	
pinch	**salt**	pinch	
1 cup	**whipping cream**, whipped	250 mL	

TOPPING:
2 cups	**cherry pie filling**, canned	500 mL	

Makes 9-12 servings.

Combine graham wafer crumbs, butter & sugar & press into a 9" (22.5 cm) square pan. Set aside in fridge.

Cream together softened cream cheese, icing sugar, vanilla & salt until fluffy. Fold into whipped cream. Spread on crumb base.

Spread cherry pie filling over all & refrigerate till serving time.

For the fruit topping, you may wish to substitute your own sweetened & thickened fresh or frozen cherries, strawberries or raspberries for the purchased pie filling.

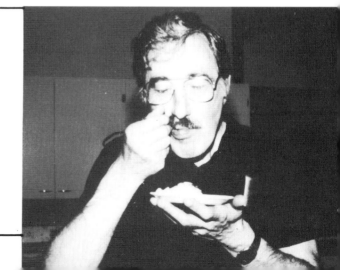

Katie Hignell is part of the Margaret Creelman Group at the West Point Grey Presbyterian Church in Vancouver. We suspect she's taken this inexpensive and easy dessert to potluck suppers on more than one occasion.

Katie Hignell's
Flora's Dessert

BASE & TOPPING:

1½ cups	**graham wafer crumbs**	375 mL
4 Tbsp	**butter**, melted	60 mL
2 Tbsp	**sugar**	30 mL

Makes 12 servings.

Combine melted butter, sugar & crumbs until well blended. Put ¼ cup (60 mL) aside for topping & press the remainder of the crumbs into the bottom of a 9" x 13" (22.5 x 32.5 cm) pan.

FILLING:

8 oz	**cream cheese**	225 g
14 oz	**crushed pineapple**, drained	398 mL
1 tsp	**vanilla**	.5 mL
½ cup	**icing sugar**	125 mL
2 env.	**dessert topping mix**	2 env.
1 cup	**milk**	250 mL

Cream the cheese, add the pineapple, vanilla & icing sugar. Whip the dessert topping and milk in a separate bowl according to package directions.

Whip the cream cheese mixture & dessert topping together. Spread over the crumb base. Sprinkle reserved ¼ cup (60 mL) of crumbs on top & refrigerate at least 1 hour.

"Spreadable" or Winnipeg cream cheese is easier to work with. For "calorie counters" make sure the pineapple is unsweetened & leave out the icing sugar. It still tastes yummy!

Take a large white fish...
Rt. Rev. Bob Smith, who is the Moderator of the United Church of Canada, has a most delightful sense of humor. Here's one of the recipes he sent. The other is on page 32. He says it's a Norwegian dish called *lutefisk*.

"Take a large white fish. Split it and remove the backbone and find a large piece of seasoned pine of sufficient width to accommodate the fish.

"Tack the fish to the board and leave the board in the sun for three months. On Christmas Eve, or on a similar festive occasion, prepare copious quantities of mashed potatoes. When everything is assembled, take the fish off the board, throw away the fish and eat the board.''

Mr. Justice George Hill and Mrs. Hill of Estevan, Saskatchewan, both enjoy church suppers in their Anglican church. There's always "a variety of good food, and the fellowship is important."

Mr. Hill is a Judge of the Queen's Bench, and, as Chancellor of the Diocese of Qu'Appelle, handles the legal aspects of the Diocese.

A very similar recipe for this attractive and tasty dessert was sent in by Ruth Baren of the United Church in Yellow Grass, Saskatchewan.

Mr. Justice George Hill and Mrs. Hill's Pistachio Almond Cheesecake

BASE:

½ cup	**butter**	125 mL
1 cup	**flour**	250 mL
½ cup	**almonds**, slivered	125 mL
½ tsp	**almond flavoring**	2 mL

Makes 12 servings.

Preheat oven to 350°F.

Blend butter, flour & almonds together with a pastry blender. (Using your fingers works even better!) It will be very stiff. Blend in almond flavoring. Press into bottom of a 9" x 13" (22.5 x 32.5 cm) pan & bake at 350°F. for 20 minutes. Cool.

CHEESE LAYER:

8 oz	**cream cheese**	225 g
1 cup	**icing sugar**	250 mL
2 Tbsp	**lemon juice**	30 mL
1 cup	**heavy cream**, whipped	250 mL

Beat cream cheese with icing sugar. Add lemon juice. Fold in whipped cream. Spread this mixture over the base. Chill until this layer partially sets—about an hour. This makes it easier to spread the third layer on top.

PISTACHIO LAYER:

2 pkgs	**pistachio instant pudding**	2 pkgs
2¾ cups	**milk**	680 mL
	whipped cream, garnish	

Whip the instant pudding & milk together 5 minutes. Spread over cheese layer & chill well—at least 4 hours or else it will "sag" when you cut it. It might also be frozen.

When ready to serve, cut into squares & top with whipped cream.

Take no thought for your life, what you shall eat, or what you shall drink.
Matthew 6:25

"This cheesecake is always the first to go at a potluck dessert party," says Janie Goodwin, the Christian Education Coordinator at the St. David's Presbyterian Church in Kelowna.

Janie's work at her church is to "encourage commitment and growth", but this deliciously decadent cheesecake which she sent us, may encourage another kind of growth. But it's worth every calorie. It's a superb cheesecake.

Those who might prefer a thin crust could use only half of the crust recipe.

Janie Goodwin's Mom's Cheesecake

CRUST:		
1 cup	**flour**	250 mL
¼ cup	**sugar**	60 mL
¼ tsp	**vanilla**	1 mL
1	**egg yolk**	1
½ cup	**soft butter**	125 mL
1 tsp	**lemon rind**, grated	5 mL

Makes 12 servings.

Preheat oven to 400°F.

Sift dry ingredients into a bowl. Make a well & into it pour egg yolk & vanilla. Add butter & lemon rind & mix thoroughly with a pastry blender or your fingers until it forms a smooth ball. Cover & chill 1 hour.

Press evenly into the bottom & halfway up the sides of a 9" (22.5 cm) springform pan. Bake at 400°F. for 8-10 minutes. Remove from oven.

FILLING:		
2-3 Tbsp	**blackberry jam** (or other variety)	30-45 mL
16 oz	**cream cheese**, softened	450 g
4	**eggs**	4
2 tsp	**vanilla**	10 mL
⅔ cup	**sugar**	170 mL
¼ tsp	**salt**	1 mL
2 Tbsp	**flour**	30 mL

Turn oven to 350°F. Spread jam on bottom crust. In bowl, beat cream cheese until smooth. Add eggs beating well after each. Add vanilla, sugar, salt & flour & blend. Pour into crust & bake at 350°F. for 45-60 minutes. Remove from oven.

TOPPING:		
1 cup	**sour cream**	250 mL
½ cup	**sugar**	125 mL

Turn oven to 450°F. Combine sour cream & sugar & mix well. Spread over filling & return to oven for 4-5 minutes. Cool.

Laura Hawthorn remembers a particularly fine church supper which took the form of a Cranberry Celebration hosted by the Gibson Indian Reserve. 200 members of the Muskoka United Church Women then toured the cranberry marsh, and, says Laura, "now we have a new interest in cranberries."

No matter what you make with cranberries, their deep red always adds a note of color to the table.

Laura Hawthorn's Cranberry Refrigerator Dessert

CRUMB LAYER:

1⅓ cups	**graham wafer crumbs**	335 mL
¼ cup	**sugar**	60 mL
¼ cup	**butter**	60 mL

FILLING:

½ cup	**butter**	125 mL
1 cup	**icing sugar**	250 mL
2	**eggs**	2

TOPPING:

2 cups	**cranberries**, fresh or frozen	500 mL
½ cup	**sugar**	125 mL
2 tsp	**unflavored gelatin**	10 mL
2 Tbsp	**cold water**	30 mL
1	**banana**	1
½ cup	**heavy cream**	125 mL

Makes 10 servings.

Combine crumbs & sugar & rub or cut in butter. Reserve 2 Tbsp (30 mL) & press remaining crumb mixture into bottom of 8" (20 cm) square pan.

Cream butter, add icing sugar, then eggs, creaming until smooth. Spread over crumb base.

Chop the cranberries, transfer to saucepan, add the sugar & let stand until liquid begins to form on bottom. Soften gelatin in cold water. Add to cranberries & simmer for several minutes until sugar & gelatin are dissolved.

Cool to room temperature, add diced banana & spread over filling. Chill thoroughly, for 3-4 hours.

When ready to serve, whip heavy cream & spread over cranberries. Sprinkle reserved crumbs on top.

A grace:

For health and strength and daily food,
We give Thee thanks, O Lord.
                    Author Unknown

It's always nice to have the dessert made ahead of time. That's only one of the advantages of this dessert from Gladys Perkins of Kelowna. It's a good dish for special occasions.

Gladys Perkins' Strawberry Angel Torte

2 Tbsp	**unflavored gelatin**	30 mL
½ cup	**cold water**	125 mL
2 cups	**strawberries**, fresh or frozen & thawed	500 mL
3 Tbsp	**lemon juice**	45 mL
1 cup	**sugar**	250 mL
¼ tsp	**salt**	1 mL
2½ cups	**heavy cream** divided	625 mL
1 large	**angel cake**	1 large

Makes 12 servings.

In top of double boiler, soften gelatin in cold water; dissolve over hot water. Crush strawberries & add to gelatin. Add lemon juice, sugar & salt. Mix, then chill until partially set.

Whip 1¾ cups (430 mL) cream; fold into strawberry mixture.

Prepare cake by cutting a 1" (2.5 cm) slice off the top, set it aside. Hollow out center of cake leaving inner & outer side walls & bottom about 5/8" (1.5 cm) thick. A fork is a handy tool for this. (The removed pieces of cake can be frozen for future use.)

Spoon the strawberry filling into the hollow & replace the top slice of cake. "Ice" torte with remaining ¾ cup (180 mL) cream, whipped, & garnish with strawberries.

Photo: Bob Greichen

People who know what it's like to go without food, sometimes remember the church suppers as one occasion, when just for a little while, "we felt like millionaires."

Perhaps that's how this dessert got its name. It comes from Rev. Bruce Balfour of the University Hill United Church in Vancouver. Certainly, eating this dessert would make you feel like a millionaire.

Bruce Balfour's Millionaire Dessert

1 small	**angel food cake**,	1 small
FILLING:		
1 Tbsp	**unflavored gelatin**	15 mL
¼ tsp	**salt**	1 mL
1½ cups	**sugar**, divided	375 mL
6	**eggs**, separated	6
¼ cup	**water**	60 mL
¾ cup	**lemon juice**	180 mL
2 tsp	**lemon rind**, grated	10 mL
TOPPING:		
1 cup	**whipping cream**	250 mL
2 Tbsp	**sugar**	30 mL
½ tsp	**vanilla**	2 mL

Makes 12 servings.

Tear cake into bite-sized pieces.

Mix gelatin, salt & ¾ cup (180 mL) sugar in top of double boiler. Beat egg yolks, water & lemon juice; blend with gelatin mixture. Cook over boiling water, stirring constantly until the gelatin is dissolved & yolk cooked, about 10 minutes.

Remove from heat & stir in rind. Chill, stirring occasionally until mixture mounds when dropped from a spoon.

Beat egg whites, gradually adding ¾ cup (180 mL) sugar until stiff. Fold in lemon mixture.

Spoon a thin layer of egg mixture into bottom of oiled angel food pan; arrange one third of the cake pieces on top of this, followed by another layer of egg mixture. Continue alternating layers, taking care that there is enough egg mixture between the cake pieces to bind them together.

Refrigerate several hours or overnight.

Turn out onto serving plate. Whip cream with sugar & vanilla until thick. "Frost" dessert with cream & serve.

Meals often have a ritual significance. For those who know the story, who are part of the tradition, sharing a meal or eating a certain dish can help us know, as Tevya says in *Fiddler on the Roof*, "who we are and what God expects us to do."

Cookbook editor Elaine Towgood offers a recipe for Haroset, which to some people would be just a fresh fruit salad. Others would recognize it as part of the Jewish Seder meal, symbolizing the mortar used for brick making while the Hebrew people were slaves in Egypt.

Elaine Towgood's Haroset

6	**apples**, peeled & cut into small chunks	6	
¼ tsp	**cinnamon**	1 mL	
¼ cup	**walnuts**, crushed	60 mL	
¾ cup	**dark raisins**	180 mL	
¼ cup	**grape juice** or **wine**	60 mL	
⅓ cup	**honey**	85 mL	

Makes 6 servings.

Sprinkle apple generously with cinnamon. Add other ingredients & mix well. Chill, covered. Serve cold.

Mr. Van der Pyl and the horseradish...

There's almost a "folk literature" of stories about things that happened at church suppers. Doug Flanders, who handles statistics for the United Church of Canada, still laughs when he tells this one.

"It was a great roast beef dinner in the Fellowship Hall of my home church, Trinity United in Ingersoll, Ontario. And it was bountiful as only such dinners can be.

"Across from us sat Mr. and Mrs. Van der Pyl, the caretakers for our church. They were good people, well liked and respected and there was much joviality around the table as the meal progressed.

"Suddenly, Mr. Van der Pyl, seeing an unfamiliar dish near his plate, said, 'What's this?' Before anyone could stop him, he dipped his spoon into the whitish substance and popped into his mouth a heaping portion of—yes, horseradish!

"You can imagine the consternation of those present, not the least of whom was Mr. Van der Pyl himself. Tears were soon streaming down his face; glasses of water were rushed to him from all sides.

"But with those tears was a face alive with mirth and his shoulders were heaving with laughter at himself. Soon everyone was laughing. And no one enjoyed the joke more than Mr. Van der Pyl, the victim."

Madeline Ingledew, who lives in Victoria, has plenty of occasions to make this light and flavorful dish. She's often baking or cooking for the Anglican Church Women at St. Dunstan's Church.

Madeline Ingledew's Rhubarb Sponge

1 env.	**unflavored gelatin**	1 env.
3 Tbsp	**cold water**	45 mL
2 cups	**stewed rhubarb** sweetened to taste	500 mL
3	**egg whites**	3

CUSTARD:

3	**egg yolks**, slightly beaten	3
¼ cup	**sugar**	60 mL
1/8 tsp	**salt**	.5 mL
2 cups	**milk**, scalded	500 mL
½ tsp	**vanilla**	2 mL

Makes 8 servings.

Soften gelatin in cold water, then add to hot rhubarb & mix until gelatin is completely dissolved. Cool thoroughly.

Beat egg whites until stiff. Fold into cooled rhubarb until thoroughly combined. Chill in fridge until set.

Combine egg yolks, sugar & salt in top of double boiler. Gradually stir in hot milk. Cook over hot (but not boiling) water until mixture coats a spoon, stirring constantly. Remove from heat & add vanilla. Chill thoroughly.

When ready to serve, spoon rhubarb sponge into dishes & top with custard.

I always try to get too much on my plate...

Skills in one area of life don't necessarily apply to other areas. Jim Taylor, author of *An Everyday God* and editor of *Currents* and **pmc** *The Practice of Ministry in Canada*, chooses words carefully, and ruthlessly weeds out anything that's not necessary to the text. But when it comes to church suppers, he does a complete reversal.

"I always try to get too much onto my plate on the first round. And on the second round.

"One dish I always find irresistible is—well, I don't know the name for it, but it always seems to appear from somewhere. Most often, it's in a big black castiron pot, and it's filled with meatballs swimming in a rich, red-brown sauce, slightly spicy, with an aroma that starts my stomach juices yearning while I'm still well back in the line."

Edith Parkyn, the organist at Trinity United in Vernon, B.C., knows what to do in the winter when fresh fruit is expensive or unavailable. She's had good success with this recipe, which has the advantage of using canned fruit.

Edith Parkyn's Peach Mallow Pie

CRUST:

1¼ cups	**graham wafer crumbs**	310 mL
¼ cup	**sugar**	60 mL
6 Tbsp	**butter**, melted	90 mL

FILLING:

2-14 oz	**peach halves,** canned	2-398 mL
⅓ cup	**peach syrup**	85 mL
⅓ cup	**orange juice**	85 mL
4 cups	**miniature marshmallows**	1 L
½ tsp	**almond extract**	2 mL
1 Tbsp	**lemon juice**	15 mL
½ cup	**whipping cream**	125 mL

Makes 8 servings.

Combine graham wafer crumbs, sugar & melted butter. Press into a buttered 9″ (22.5 cm) pie plate. Chill in fridge while preparing filling.

Set peaches in colander to drain, saving syrup.

Combine syrup, orange juice & marshmallows in top of double boiler. Set over boiling water till marshmallows are barely melted, stirring constantly. Remove from heat. Add almond extract & lemon juice. Chill in fridge till slightly thickened.

Beat whipping cream till stiff & fold into chilled marshmallow mixture.

Arrange peach halves on crust, saving one or two for garnish. Pour marshmallow mixture over peaches; slice remaining peach & garnish top of pie.

Chill 2-3 hours until set.

We never repent of having eaten too little.
                       Thomas Jefferson

Wolly Brons of Enderby, B.C., once heard someone at a church supper say, "you know, you can eat all you want at a church supper, because food for the soul has no calories."

This recipe has calories, unfortunately, but it's light and delicious, and often requested at events catered to by the St. Andrew's United Church Women. And it's convenient because you can make it ahead of time.

Similar recipes were sent in by Esther Faubert of Sicamous, B.C., and Ruth Baren of Yellow Grass, Saskatchewan.

Wolly Brons' Lemon Delight

Serves at least 12.

BASE:

2 cups	graham wafer crumbs	500 mL
⅓ cup	sugar	85 mL
½ cup	butter, melted	125 mL

Mix graham wafer crumbs with sugar; add melted butter & press half this mixture into a 9" x 13" (22.5 x 32.5 cm) pan.

FILLING:

3½ oz	lemon gelatin, pkg	85 g
1 cup	water, boiling	250 mL
⅓ cup	sugar	85 mL
16 oz	canned milk, (well chilled)	385 mL
4 Tbsp	lemon juice	60 mL
1 Tbsp	lemon rind, grated	15 mL
pinch	salt	pinch

Dissolve gelatin in boiling water, add ⅓ cup (85 mL) sugar & stir till dissolved. Chill till *slightly* thickened (consistency of egg whites). Meanwhile, with electric mixer, whip canned milk; lastly add lemon juice & rind. Fold thickened lemon gelatin into whipped milk & pour over crumbs. Lightly sprinkle remaining crumbs over gelatin mixture & refrigerate for several hours or overnight.

*You may substitute raspberry gelatin for a different taste & color.

Ivory Snow and mashed potatoes...

People often marvel at the efficiency and team work of church suppers. But things don't always work out well.

Pegeen McAskill of Vancouver remembers one occasion when the Ivory Snow got mixed up with the powdered mashed potatoes. And my, but the potatoes whipped up nicely!

Often at church potluck suppers, people say, "isn't it wonderful how there's always a nice balance of dishes at these potlucks." Well, it isn't always that way.

Betty Mittler of Bethel United Church in Marmora, Ontario, says that at one annual meeting dinner, "this was the only dish that was not baked beans. At the next annual dinner, nobody brought baked beans!"

This light and colorful dessert would fit in nicely with a Christmas theme.

Betty Mittler's
Charlotte Joynt's
Marshmallow Squares

BASE:
¾ cup	**butter**	180 mL
⅓ cup	**brown sugar**	85 mL
1½ cup	**flour**	375 mL

FILLING:
2 Tbsp	**unflavored gelatin**	30 mL
½ cup	**cold water**	125 mL
2 cups	**sugar**	500 mL
½ cup	**hot water**	125 mL
½ cup	**maraschino cherries**, drained & chopped	125 mL
½ cup	**almonds** or **walnuts**, chopped	125 mL
1 tsp	**almond flavoring**	5 mL
few drops	red or green **food coloring**	few drops

Makes 12 servings.

Preheat oven to 325°F.

Cream butter, add brown sugar & flour & mix well. Press into an ungreased 9″ x 13″ (22.5 x 32.5 cm) pan, covering the bottom only. Prick with a fork & bake 30 minutes at 325°F. Cool completely.

Soften gelatin in ½ cup (125 mL) cold water. Combine sugar & hot water in a saucepan. Boil for 2 minutes. Add dissolved gelatin to hot syrup. Beat until stiff with an electric beater.

Add cherries, almonds, flavoring & coloring. Pour over shortbread base. Cool in refrigerator until chilled.

A grace:

"Lord, fill my mouth with worthwhile stuff,
And stop me when I've had enough!"

Author Unknown

If you're going to have a gang over for dinner, here's a suggestion from Viola Manery, who is active in the Keremeos Anglican Church Women.

This dessert is rich in flavor, light in texture, and can also be made with raspberries.

Viola Manery's Strawberry Slice

1 lb	**marshmallows**	450 g
1 cup	**milk**	250 mL
1½ cups	**sliced strawberries** fresh or frozen	375 mL
1 cup	**heavy cream**, whipped	250 mL
	berries & cream, garnish	

Makes 24 servings.

Melt marshmallows with milk over boiling water in the top of a double boiler. Stir until smooth. Remove from heat & set over ice water. Cool mixture until it begins to gel. (If you aren't in a hurry, cool mixture in the refrigerator.)

Add berries, then fold in whipped cream. Pour into a 9" x 13" (22.5 x 32.5 cm) pan & chill several hours to set. Cut into squares & serve with a dollop of whipped cream & a few berries.

Eighteen pans of cabbage rolls...

Church groups across the country have a long and colorful history of "catering" for everything from service club meetings to weddings and funerals. That called for lots of hard work, but sometimes also some fast thinking.

Gwendolyn Mills of Meadow Lake, (she's the Saskatchewan co-ordinator of the United Church Women) tells one such story.

"It was a hot, July afternoon. The guests were arriving and the ladies were scurrying about putting last minute items on the tables which would seat 200 guests. The kitchen was filled with food of every sort, and the air was filled with the tension and mild panic that comes when not everything is working out just as it should.

"Complaints were being muttered by some of the ladies about there being 'nowhere to put anything' or 'I know it's here, but I can't find a thing with all this stuff piled around.'

"The baker chose the worst moment to arrive with two huge pans of cabbage rolls and the announcement, 'I have eighteen pans of them.'

"There was a moment of dead silence. Then the lady in charge of the catering broke the tension by saying, 'Well, just hold them for a minute. We'll build a new wing onto the kitchen.''

Beryl Dalgliesh of Kelowna remembers church suppers as being very "warm, loving, happy, noisy gatherings packed to the doors." Now, she often finds herself baking a pie and working at the church suppers in St. Paul's United Church in Kelowna.

A very similar recipe was sent to us by Ethel Buck of Vancouver. It's a pleasantly spiced version of the classic pumpkin pie.

Beryl Dalgliesh's Pumpkin Pie

1½ cups	**pumpkin**, canned or cooked & mashed	375 mL	
¾ cup	**sugar**	180 mL	
½ tsp	**salt**	2 mL	
1 tsp	**cinnamon**	5 mL	
¾ tsp	**ginger**	4 mL	
¼ tsp	**nutmeg**	1 mL	
¼ tsp	**cloves**	1 mL	
3	**eggs**, slightly beaten	3	
1¼ cups	**milk**	310 mL	
6 oz	**evaporated milk**, tin	170 mL	
1-10″	**unbaked pastry shell**	1-25 cm	
	whipped cream, garnish		

Makes 8 servings.

Preheat oven to 400°F.

Thoroughly combine the pumpkin, sugar, salt & spices. Blend in eggs, milk & evaporated milk.

Pour into unbaked pastry shell (have edges crimped high—filling is generous).

Bake at 400°F. for 50 minutes, or until knife inserted halfway between center & outside comes out clean. Cool.

Serve with whipped cream & a dash of nutmeg.

The halls of the professor and the philosopher are deserted, but what a crowd there is in the cafes!

Seneca

Mike Chepesuik of Kelowna has a problem. He loves his wife's lemon pie. He's also polite. So whenever there's a church supper, he lets others get ahead of him in the line-up at the dessert table. Which is nice, except that the lemon pie is all gone before he gets any.

This recipe, from editor Elaine Towgood, is dedicated to him.

Mike Chepesuik's Lemon Pie

9"	baked pie shell	22.5 cm
FILLING:		
1 cup	sugar	250 mL
3 Tbsp	flour	45 mL
3 Tbsp	cornstarch	45 mL
1/8 tsp	salt	.5 mL
1½ cups	boiling water	375 mL
2	egg yolks, beaten	2
1 Tbsp	butter	15 mL
¼ cup	lemon juice	60 mL
2 tsp	lemon rind, finely grated	30 mL
MERINGUE:		
2	egg whites	2
¼ tsp	cream of tartar	1 mL
4 Tbsp	sugar	60 mL
¼ tsp	vanilla	1 mL

Makes 6 servings.

Combine sugar, flour, cornstarch & salt in top of double boiler. Gradually stir in boiling water. Place over *direct* heat & bring to a boil, stirring constantly.

Then place pot over boiling water, cooking for an additional 5 minutes.

Pour some of the hot mixture over beaten egg yolks &, when mixed, return all to pan to cook over boiling water for another 2 minutes, stirring constantly.

Remove from heat & blend in butter, lemon juice & lemon rind. Cool slightly. Pour into baked pie shell.

Preheat oven to 400ºF.

Beat egg whites & cream of tartar to very soft peaks. Gradually add sugar, one tablespoon at a time, & continue beating until stiff & all sugar is dissolved. Beat in vanilla.

Pile meringue on warm pie filling, making sure to spread to the edges to prevent shrinking.

Bake at 400ºF. for 7-8 minutes, or until lightly browned. Cool on rack away from drafts. Serve at room temperature.

Ralph Milton, author of *This United Church of Ours*, has been searching for years, trying to find the kind of rhubarb pie his mother used to make out in Horndean, Manitoba; a pie that used eggs in the recipe to reduce the acidity and give it a more subtle flavor.

Here's just such a recipe from Irene Hallisey of St. Pius X Catholic Church in Kelowna.

We're tempted to dedicate this recipe to Rev. Bill Steadman of Forest, Ontario, who is still in mourning over the time when they allowed seconds in pies, but ran out.

Irene Hallisey's Rhubarb Custard Pie

	pastry for 10″ (25 cm) pie	
2	**eggs**	2
1¾ cups	**sugar**	430 mL
¼ cup	**flour**	60 mL
¼ tsp	**mace**	1 mL
pinch	**salt**	pinch
¼ cup	**orange juice**	60 mL
4 cups	**rhubarb**, chopped	1 L
1 Tbsp	**butter**, melted	15 mL

Makes 8 servings.

Preheat oven to 400°F.

Line pie plate with pastry. Prepare strips of pastry for lattice top.

In a large bowl, beat eggs slightly; blend in sugar, flour, mace, salt & orange juice. Stir in rhubarb; coating pieces well with egg mixture.

Spoon into pastry shell. Arrange pastry strips as a lattice on top. Brush top lightly with melted butter. Bake at 400°F. for 15 minutes, reduce temperature to 375°F. & continue cooking for 35 minutes.

She disapproved of the song...
Rev. Philip Cline, of Toronto, remembers church suppers in Zelma, Saskatchewan.

"The annual 'Fowl Supper' was sponsored by the ladies of our United Church. It was always held in the community hall, with entertainment following provided by members of the community and the school children.

"I remember one occasion when I sang a duet with a girl named Johanna Fisher. We sang, 'Little Brown Jug'.

"My mother, a staunch member of the Ladies Aid, was faced with a serious quandary. She was certainly proud of her nine-year-old son and his singing. But oh, how she disapproved of the song and its content!"

Bonnie Brennan who loves people and food in that order, asked that a good recipe for raisin pie be included in this book. Bonnie has served the church for many years. Currently, she's in charge of almost everything at Canadian Conference of Catholic Bishops office in Ottawa.

The orange juice and rind make this raisin pie an especially good one.

Bonnie Brennan's Raisin Pie

2 cups	**raisins**	500 mL
1¼ cups	**water**	310 mL
½ cup	**orange juice**	125 mL
½ cup	**brown sugar**	125 mL
2 Tbsp	**cornstarch**	30 mL
1 tsp	**cinnamon**	5 mL
1 tsp	**orange rind**	5 mL
1/8 tsp	**salt**	.5 mL
¼ cup	**water**	60 mL
1 Tbsp	**vinegar**	15 mL
2 Tbsp	**butter**	30 mL
	pastry for a 9" (22.5 cm) pie	

Makes 6 servings.

Preheat oven to 425°F.

Boil raisins with 1¼ cups (310 mL) water & orange juice for 5 minutes in a covered saucepan.

Combine brown sugar, cornstarch, cinnamon, orange rind & salt with the ¼ cup (60 mL) water. Add to cooked raisins. Bring to a full boil, stirring constantly.

Remove from heat. Add vinegar & butter. Line pie plate with pastry. Pour raisins into pie shell. Cover with pastry top, making several steam slits.

Bake at 425°F. for 45 minutes or until bottom pastry is browned. Serve warm with ice cream.

> He that banquets every day never makes a good meal.
> — Thomas Fuller

For a few short weeks each year, fresh peaches are available at a relatively reasonable price. That's a good time to make a half-dozen of these pies. Or more.

This recipe came to us from Catherine Craig of St. Ann's Catholic Church in Abbotsford, B.C. A similar recipe, except that it used strawberries, came from Margaret Schneider of Meadow Lake, Saskatchewan. Our editors point out that you can also use this recipe with raspberries or blueberries.

Catherine Craig's Fresh Peach Pie

9"	**baked pie shell**	22.5 cm
7-8	**peaches**, large	7-8
1 cup	**sugar**	250 mL
4 Tbsp	**cornstarch**	60 mL
1 cup	**whipping cream**	250 mL

Serves 6.

Finely chop enough fresh peaches to measure 1½ cups (375 mL). Mix sugar & cornstarch in medium saucepan & stir in chopped peaches. Cook over medium heat, stirring constantly, till mixture thickens & boils. Reduce heat & continue cooking for 10 minutes. Remove from heat & allow to cool.

Slice remaining peaches & layer in pie shell alternately with cooked mixture, beginning & ending with mixture. Refrigerate at least 4 hours.

Before serving, top with whipped cream.

Photo: Berkeley Studio

Not with whom thou art bred, but with whom thou art fed.

        Cervantes

Anna Pavlova was a famous Russian Ballerina, noted for her interpretation of *Swan Lake*. We assume the lightness of the meringue reminded the New Zealanders, who first developed this recipe, of the lightness of the famous dancer.

The recipe came from Margaret Lawson, of Don Mills, Ontario, who said "It's a favorite with my Tuesday Study Group."

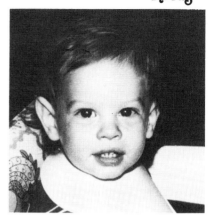

Margaret Lawson's Pavlova

3	**egg whites**	3
1/8 tsp	**salt**	.5 mL
1 tsp	**vinegar**	5 mL
1 cup	**sugar**	250 mL
	whipped cream & **fruit**, to garnish	

Makes 8 servings.

Preheat oven to 250°F.

Lightly grease a cookie sheet, cover with tin foil & grease that as well.

Beat egg whites & salt on high till foamy. Add vinegar & beat well. Gradually add sugar, a spoonful at a time, till egg whites are thick & glossy & sugar is completely dissolved.

Spread in a circle (approximately 9" - 22.5 cm) on tin foil making a dome shape. With back of spoon, make a slight depression in top of meringue.

Bake at 250°F. for 1½ hours. Leave in oven to cool.

To serve, cover Pavlova with whipped cream & fresh fruit.

A row over peas and carrots...
Not all memories of church suppers are happy ones. Dr. Garth Mundle, the Principal of St. Stephen's College in Edmonton, remembers the early days of ministry when "a dreadful row developed over whether peas or carrots would be served at the annual fall supper. As I recall, two or three families 'left' the church over the matter. I remember muttering to myself, 'they were good at raising money and raising hell'."

In the days when wood stoves made heating up the oven a major production, meals were planned so that several things could be done in that oven at the same time. Nowadays heating up an oven is "no big deal", but those who are energy conscious still try to do several things at one time. That's one big advantage of this self-saucing cake. You can put it in the oven and bake it with the rest of the dinner.

The recipe comes to us from Ruth Bell of Deloraine, Manitoba, and from Madeline Ingledew of Victoria.

Madeline and Ruth's Chocolate Upside-Down Pudding

CAKE:
¼ cup	**butter**	60 mL
¾ cup	**sugar**	180 mL
1 tsp	**vanilla**	5 mL
1½ cups	**flour**	375 mL
2½ tsp	**baking powder**	12 mL
2 Tbsp	**cocoa**	30 mL
¼ tsp	**salt**	1 mL
¾ cup	**milk**	180 mL
½ cup	**nuts**, chopped	125 mL

TOPPING:
¼ cup	**cocoa**	60 mL
1 cup	**brown sugar**	250 mL
1 cup	**boiling water**	250 mL

Makes 9 servings.

Preheat oven to 350°F.

Cream butter & sugar, add vanilla. Sift flour, baking powder, cocoa & salt together. Add to creamed mixture alternately with milk. Stir in nuts.

Pour into a greased 8" x 8" (20 x 20 cm) cake pan.

Mix together cocoa & brown sugar. Spread over cake mixture, then pour 1 cup (250 mL) boiling water over all.

Bake uncovered at 350°F. for 45 minutes.

Rolls of paper-wrapped ice cream

"My strongest memories of church suppers," says Muriel Duncan of Toronto, "seem to be those Sunday School picnics." Muriel, who is now Managing Editor of the United Church Observer, describes her memories with obvious relish.

"We ate at wooden tables on the shores of Lake Huron, after an afternoon of swimming, three-legged races and guess-how-many-beans-in-the-jar contests, and before the softball games among the children and the farmers who'd stolen an afternoon from haying.

"Lemonade was dipped from tall cream pails, sandwiches were shared, and best of all, rolls of paper-wrapped vanilla ice cream were passed out to everyone."

Rhoda Stein, Editor of *BC Image*, is also a member of the choir at West Burnaby United Church. She enjoys many things, among them Scottish trifle. This recipe came to Rhoda from a Scottish friend who came to Canada to share the good things of her homeland.

Rhoda Stein's Scottish Trifle

2 cups	**custard pudding,*** thin	500 mL
3 oz	**raspberry gelatin**, pkg.	85 g
1	**white cake**, small, preferably day-old	1
14 oz	**fruit cocktail**, can	398 mL
1 cup	**whipped cream**	250 mL

Makes 8-10 servings.

Prepare thin custard according to directions on tin of custard powder or use recipe on page 121. Set aside to cool.

Prepare gelatin according to package directions & allow to chill until *partially* set.

Slice cake into pieces about ½" (1 cm) thick. Use as many pieces as necessary to line bottom & sides of glass or china serving bowl.

Pour syrup from fruit cocktail evenly over cake, soaking each piece. Spoon fruit over base of cake. Pour custard evenly over all, including sides. Spoon partially-set gelatin over custard & fruit. Lastly, decorate with whipped cream around edges.

Chill trifle in fridge several hours before serving so cake absorbs juice & custard. Serve chilled.

*Use custard recipe from "Rhubarb Sponge," page 121.

To lengthen thy life, lessen thy meals.

Benjamin Franklin

It must have been quite a time at St. Dunstan's Anglican Church in Victoria. Jean Smith tells about the day they had a "make-your-own-crepe" party. "Everybody brought fillings such as chicken, potato, sour cream, fruit, etc. We put up six or eight frying pans, and everyone made their own crepe." Part of the fun was having people flip the pancake in the pan and race across the gym. It must have been fun for everyone except the poor soul who had to clean the floor.

This simple recipe can be halved.

Dianne Friesen probably wasn't at the St. Dunstan's shindig, because she lives in Winfield, B.C. But if she had been, Dianne would have brought her Mocha Mousse filling, which turns a simple crepe into something delightfully decadent."

Jean Smith's Easy Crepes

1 cup	cold water	250 mL
1 cup	cold milk	250 mL
4	eggs	4
½ tsp	salt	2 mL
2 cups	flour	500 mL
2 Tbsp	butter, melted	30 mL

Makes about 24 crepes.

Put all ingredients in a blender; blend 2 minutes. Refrigerate for 2 hours.

Heat a small nonstick frying pan over medium heat till water drops bounce on the surface.

Pour approx. 2 Tbsp (30 mL) of the batter into pan & swirl to make thin circle. Cook about 30 seconds, or till the edges are dry. Turn crepe & cook reverse side till lightly browned. Continue cooking one at a time until batter is used up.

Cool crepes on rack, separating each with waxed paper. They may be wrapped & frozen at this time for future use.

Dianne Friesen's Mocha Mousse Filling

6 oz	chocolate chips	175 g
¼ cup	coffee, very hot	60 mL
2 Tbsp	coffee-flavored liquer	30 mL
4	egg yolks	4
4	egg whites	4
¼ cup	sugar	60 mL
½ cup	whipping cream	125 mL
	whipped cream & chocolate sprinkles to garnish.	

"Fills" about 2 dozen crepes.

Combine chocolate chips & *hot* coffee in blender. Blend until smooth. Add liquer & egg yolks & blend for 30 seconds on high. Pour into mixing bowl.

In a large glass bowl, beat egg whites to soft peaks. Gradually beat in sugar till stiff. Fold into chocolate mixture. Whip cream & fold into above. Chill thoroughly.

Fill each crepe with 2-3 Tbsp of chocolate mousse. Decorate with additional whipped cream & sprinkles.

A grace...

*God of love,
you love us all.
You want all your people,
of every race and tribe and nation
to live together
in justice and in love.
May this food we share
express our unity
with sisters and brothers
throughout the world.
May this food strengthen our bodies;
may this fellowship strengthen our faith,
so that we may be your purpose
in every part
of our everyday living.
Amen.*

Few people are neutral about Dr. Garth Mundle, Principal of St. Stephen's College in Edmonton. Many people love him. A few don't.

Garth rides his motorcycle to work. And these rolls are specially formulated to be eaten while riding a motorcycle.

These rolls are made like cinnamon rolls, but they have a tangy orange flavor. They also freeze well, which is handy if you're going to eat them riding a motorcycle in Edmonton.

Garth Mundle's Motorcycle Rolls

1 Tbsp	**yeast**	15 mL
1 tsp	**sugar**	5 mL
1 cup	**warm water**	250 mL
1 cup	**sugar**	250 mL
¼ cup	**butter**	60 mL
1 tsp	**salt**	5 mL
1 cup	**hot water**	250 mL
1	**egg**, beaten	1
6 cups	**flour**	1.5 L
4 Tbsp	**soft butter**	60 mL
3 Tbsp	**orange rind**, grated	45 mL
1 cup	**sugar**	250 mL

Makes about 30 rolls.

Dissolve yeast with 1 tsp (5 mL) sugar in 1 cup (250 mL) warm water. Let stand 10 minutes.

In a large bowl, dissolve 1 cup (250 mL) sugar, ¼ cup (60 mL) butter & salt in 1 cup (250 mL) *hot* water. Cool to lukewarm then add beaten egg. Add the yeast & water, then 3 cups (750 mL) flour. Beat well.

Add remaining flour or as much as is needed to make a soft dough. Knead until smooth. Let rise in a warm place 2 hours or until doubled in bulk.

Mix grated orange rind & and sugar.

Punch down risen dough & divide into 2 halves. Roll (or press with fingers) each half into a rectangle about 10" x 15" (25 x 37.5 cm). Spread with butter, then sprinkle with orange/sugar mixture. Roll up like a jelly roll.

Cut into approximately 1" (2.5 cm) lengths & place in greased muffin tins or side by side in shallow cake pans. Let rise about 1 hour or until light.

Bake at 350°F. for 20 minutes.

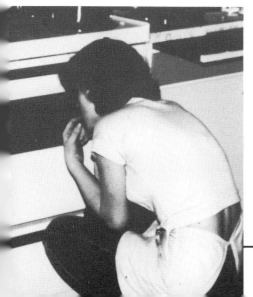

If you need hot rolls for dinner, here's something you can whip up in no time. The recipe comes from Connie Bickford of South Burnaby United Church. A similar recipe came from Mrs. Bert Topham of Grandview, Manitoba.

Connie Bickford's
Rapid Rolls

4-5 cups	**flour**, divided	1-1.25 L
2 Tbsp	**sugar**	30 mL
2 tsp	**salt**	10 mL
1 Tbsp	**active dry yeast**	15 mL
2 Tbsp	**butter**, softened	30 mL
2 cups	**hot water**	500 mL
1	**egg white**, room temperature	1
2 Tbsp	**corn meal**	30 mL

Makes 24 rolls.

In large bowl, thoroughly mix 1 cup (250 mL) flour, sugar, salt & undissolved yeast. Add butter. Gradually add very hot tap water to dry ingredients & beat 2 minutes at medium speed.

Add egg white & 1 cup (250 mL) more flour. Beat at medium speed for 1 minute, scraping bowl often. With mixing spoon stir in additional flour to make a soft dough.

Turn out onto lightly-floured surface & knead until smooth, about 8-10 minutes. Place in warm greased bowl, turning to grease top. Cover with cloth, let rise in warm place until doubled, about 45 minutes.

Punch dough down; turn out onto counter or board; cover, let rest 10 minutes. Divide dough in half. Form each half into a roll, cut into 12 pieces; form each into a smooth ball. Place about 3" (7.5 cm) apart on greased baking sheets which have been sprinkled with cornmeal.

Cover, let rise until doubled, about 45 minutes. Bake at 375°F. for 15 minutes or until nicely browned. Remove from baking sheets & let cool on racks.

They have digged their grave with their teeth.
                        Thomas Adams

This is neither a yeast nor a baking powder dough. It's easy to make and results in a moist, fine-textured roll. It can be turned into cinnamon buns with the addition of 1 tsp (5 mL) of cinnamon and 1 cup (250 mL) of raisins.

The recipe came to us from Barbara Ferris of Kelowna, B.C.

Barbara Ferris' German Buns

DOUGH:

4 cups	flour	1 L
1 tsp	salt	5 mL
1 cup	sugar	250 mL
1 tsp	baking soda	5 mL
1 tsp	cream of tartar	5 mL
½ cup	butter	125 mL
½ cup	lard	125 mL
1	egg	1
1¾ cups	milk	430 mL

FILLING:

½ cup	flour	125 mL
1 cup	brown sugar	250 mL
1	egg	1

Makes 36 buns.

Sift flour, salt, sugar, baking soda & cream of tartar together into a bowl. Cut in butter & lard. Make a well in this mixture & into it pour the egg & milk. Mix quickly with a fork.

Stir flour & brown sugar together. Add egg & mix well.

Divide the dough in half. On a lightly floured board, roll or pat each piece out to a rectangle approx. 9" x 18" (22.5 x 45 cm). Spread half the filling on each piece, then roll up as you would for a jelly roll to make an 18" (45 cm) roll.

Cut roll into 1" (2.5 cm) lengths by slipping a thread under the roll, bringing the ends up & crossing them over the top, then pulling as if to tie until thread has cut through all the layers of dough.

Place on their sides 2" (5 cm) apart on greased baking sheet. Bake at 400°F. for 15-20 minutes or until light brown.

There's a Thrift Shop operated by the United Church in Winfield B.C. Providing the brains and the enthusiasm for it is Audrey Leonard, who sent us this recipe.

When you make it, be sure to use *instant* fast-rising yeast, or you'll wind up with a year's supply of hockey pucks.

Audrey Leonard's Instant Yeast Buns

3 cups	**warm water**	750 mL
⅓ cup	**sugar**	85 mL
6 Tbsp	**oil**	90 mL
1½ tsp	**salt**	7 mL
2 Tbsp	**instant fast-rising yeast**	30 mL
2	**eggs**	2
7 cups	**flour**	1.75 L

Makes about 4 dozen.

Combine in a large bowl water, sugar, oil, salt, yeast & eggs. Add 3 cups (750 mL) of flour & beat well. Gradually add remaining flour to make a soft dough.

Turn out on board & knead well about 5 minutes. Put dough in large greased bowl in a warm place. Let rise 15 minutes; punch down. Allow to rise a second time for 15 minutes; punch down. Allow to rise a third time for 20 minutes, punch down & form into buns, placing them on greased pans.

Preheat oven to 350ºF.

Allow to rise until doubled in bulk—15 minutes.

Bake at 350ºF. for 15-20 minutes.

Variation: To make whole-wheat rolls, substitute 2 cups (500 mL) whole-wheat flour for 2 cups (500 mL) white flour.

Just a little bit snug...
Janie Goodwin, who is Christian Education Coordinator at St. David's Presbyterian Church in Kelowna, remembers church suppers being just a bit snug.

"One church I worked for in New Westminster could just fit the three long tables they needed into the hall. The food would be set at one end of each table, and the minister would direct people to stand and start walking around their table. As you passed the food your plate was filled, and then you stayed in line until you got back to your place. What a system!"

Editing a cookbook had various effects on Elaine Towgood's family. Her son Paul was the most popular person in school at lunch time, because he always had something tasty to share; something his mother was currently testing.

This recipe, which comes from Lee Maranchuck of Rutland, B.C., brought instant popularity to Paul. It would be great to prepare for a youth group or Sunday School event. It's a *large* recipe.

Lee Maranchuck's Spudnuts

2 Tbsp	**yeast**	30 mL
4 cups	**milk**, scalded & cooled to lukewarm	1 L
1½ tsp	**salt**	7 mL
1 cup	**butter**, softened	250 mL
5	**eggs**, well-beaten	5
1 cup	**sugar**	250 mL
2 tsp	**nutmeg**	10 mL
2 cups	**mashed potatoes**	500 mL
14-16 cups	**flour**	3.5-4 L

Makes lots!—about 9 dozen.

In a very large bowl, combine yeast, milk, salt, soft butter, eggs, sugar & nutmeg. If the mashed potatoes are cold, add some of the liquid to them & soften with a fork or potato masher until smooth. Combine with the yeast mixture.

Add approximately 5 cups (1.25 L) flour to the yeast mixture & beat until smooth. Continue to add flour to make a soft dough. Knead well.

Put dough in large greased bowl in a warm place & allow to rise until doubled in bulk (about 1 hour); then punch down. Allow to rise a second time (about 40 minutes); punch down.

Working with about ¼ of the dough at a time on a well-floured board, roll out to about ¾" (1.5 cm) thickness & cut out with doughnut cutter.

Allow spudnuts to rise on greased or floured surfaces* until desired height (they will puff up more in cooking). Deep fry in several inches of hot oil (375°F.), turning to cook until golden on both sides.

Cool on paper towels. May be dipped in sugar or glazed while still warm.

*It's not necessary to use baking pans for rising as they will not be cooked on these — plastic is fine. I found that by the time I had finished cutting out the last spudnut, the first ones were ready to fry.

This is a very special recipe. It is sometimes referred to as Holy Bread or Urbaan. Phyllis McCallum and Walter Farquharson of Saltcoats, Saskatchewan, sent along a history and a story about this bread, which you can see on the opposite page.

These flattish buns are basically a plain, unsweetened raised bun. They are tasty on their own, but are also good with butter and cheese or jam. Kids love them!

Dr. Bill Taylor of Vancouver suggested we include a recipe for chapattis. These are not chapattis, but they are very similar.

Phyllis McCallum's Talami

1 Tbsp	**instant fast-rising yeast**	15 mL
5 cups	**flour**	1.25 L
2 tsp	**salt**	10 mL
¼ cup	**oil**	60 mL
1¾ cups	**warm water**	430 mL

Makes about 30 Talami.

In large mixing bowl combine yeast, flour & salt. Make a well in the center.

Add oil to warm (not hot) water in measuring cup. Pour into center of dry ingredients. Stir with wooden spoon till liquids are absorbed; work any remaining flour in with hands.

Turn out onto lightly-floured surface & knead gently until dough is a smooth ball (about 5 minutes). Place dough into greased bowl, cover & let rise 1 hour.

Punch dough down & break off small pieces (about the size of golf balls) & work into smooth balls. Place on lightly-floured surface, cover & allow to rise for 30 minutes.

Preheat oven to 450ºF. Place a stainless steel or cast iron flat pan on bottom rack of oven to preheat. (A cookie sheet will do).

Wet hands with water &, with finger tips, press dough as flat as possible. Place about 6 talami on cookie sheet & bake 8-10 minutes, or until lightly browned. Remove from oven & cool on rack.

Transfer remaining talami, 6 at a time, onto heated cookie sheet & bake.

Bread of Life

"This is the oldest bread in the world," says Phyllis McCallum. "It is the ancient bread of the fertile crescent of the Middle East—Syria, Lebanon, Iraq, etc.

"Originally, it may have been unleavened bread, though today most recipes use yeast. It was particularly useful in the Middle East because the nomadic tribes found it easy to make outside on flat stones or flat metal sheets over open fires. Because the loaves are flat, they are easily packed for travel and because they are cooked right through, they are well preserved.

"In all likelihood this is the same bread as was used by Jesus and the disciples; the bread that was broken at the Last Supper. It is often called Holy Bread or Urbaan, and it is offered at Holy Communion in the Orthodox Church in the Middle East. The bread is also served at Easter for breakfast with olives and yogurt."

Walter Farquharson, the minister at Phyllis' church, had a few words to add.

"A few years ago, Phyllis baked talami for our congregation to have for a special service on the Sunday following Easter. We read from Luke 24 of the journey of two disheartened and confused disciples travelling from Jerusalem to Emmaus.

"The risen Christ meets them, walks with them as a stranger and then is known to them—in the breaking of bread.

"In our worship, people shared with two or three others, something of their 'walk', their anxieties, fears, confusions, hurts. They also talked of those who, walking with them, gave them hope, faith and some sense of purpose.

"We then broke bread. The left-over talami was taken to other family members or friends not at the service. The celebration has become something we all look forward to every year. Each year Phyllis bakes the bread—about twenty loaves. One year she baked enough for us to use at a meeting of the Saskatchewan Conference of the United Church!"

We served a Passover meal...

The tradition of eating together to share a heritage of faith goes back into antiquity. Jewish people celebrate the Passover feast each year to remember their liberation from slavery. And Christians carry that tradition on in the eucharist, communion or mass.

Rev. Betty Griffiths-Ling of Shediac, New Brunswick, recalls just such an event. "When I served with the Methodist Church in England in 1980, our congregation decided to do something different at Easter time. On Maundy Thursday—the Thursday before Good Friday—we served a Passover meal, as near to the original as we could discover. This was followed by our Christian Lord's Supper.

"It was a moving and wonderfully inspiring evening, and one I shall never forget, as it brought together the two great religious rites of our Christian heritage."

If there is such a thing as a 100 percent Canadian recipe, it would certainly be bannock. This recipe comes to us from Ellen Link of Kelowna, who had it given to her by her grandmother, who received it from an Indian friend.

This biscuit was a staple among the early settlers, and it's still enjoyed around the fire at church camps, cooked over the open fire on a green stick. It's great fun to make on a family camping trip. And it's delicious eaten warm with butter and jam.

(Currants or raisins may be worked into the dough when kneading.)

This recipe is easily halved.

Ellen Link's Bannock

4 cups	**flour**	1 L
4 Tbsp	**baking powder**	60 mL
1 tsp	**salt**	5 mL
1 tsp	**sugar**	5 mL
1½ cups	**lukewarm water**	375 mL
½ cup	**oil** or **shortening,** melted	125 mL
1	**egg** (optional)	1

Preheat oven to 425°F.

Stir flour, baking powder, salt & sugar together in a large bowl. Make a well in center.

Measure warm water into a glass measuring cup & add melted shortening. An egg may be added, if desired. Stir well & pour into dry ingredients.

Mix till well combined & turn out onto lightly-floured surface. Knead gently about 5 times. Roll out & pat into 2 circles. Prick with a fork.

Place on cookie sheet & bake at 425°F. about 20 minutes. Cut in wedges.

Always a pie-eating contest...

Mrs. M. Mills of Georgetown, Ontario, remembers the big job it was to scrub out the shed for the church supper. That's where they kept the horses all winter, so it was given "a thorough cleaning and the floor given a coating of fresh-smelling sawdust. Tables were set up. They were really long boards set on sawhorses for the tables and on blocks of wood from the woodpile for the seats. There was always a pie-eating contest for the teenage boys. And if we ran out of food, someone would head for the store to buy a roll of bologna."

When, time after time, you take large batches of scones to church suppers, and there's never any left, you get the message. Peggy Henderson got the message, which is why she sent us this recipe. She's active in the Presbyterian Women's Missionary Society in Lucknow, Ontario.

Agnes Cunningham of Kelowna, B.C., and Muriel Arnold of Sicamous, B.C., sent similar recipes. This basic recipe has endless possibilities for variations. We're offering two.

Peggy Henderson's Drop Biscuits

4 cups	flour	1 L
8 tsp	baking powder	40 mL
1 tsp	salt	5 mL
1 cup	sugar	250 mL
1 cup	shortening	250 mL
2 cups	*milk	500 mL

Makes 24 biscuits.

Preheat oven to 425°F.

Sift flour, baking powder, salt & sugar into a bowl. Add shortening & cut in with pastry blender. (This mixture can be stored covered, but not refrigerated until you wish to make scones).

Add the milk & stir in with a fork. Drop from a spoon into 24 muffin tins, well greased.

Bake at 425°F. for 15 minutes or until light brown.

*2 cups (500 mL) water plus 1 cup (250 mL) milk powder can be substituted for milk.

Variations:

Raisin Biscuits: Reduce milk to 1½ cups (375 mL), add ½ cup (125 mL) raisins. Knead dough about 6 times, roll out to ¾" (1.5 cm) & cut into triangles. Bake on ungreased cookie sheet at 425°F. for 15 minutes.

Rich Scones: Reduce milk to 1 cup (250 mL), stir in 2 slightly beaten eggs & follow directions for Raisin Biscuits.

People, good wine, and Laura Hawthorn's muffins improve with age. That's not totally true, of course, but Laura's muffins at least are better on the second day.

They're worth a try, as are the muffins from Elaine Towgood's innovative kitchen.

Elaine Towgood's Cheddar Bacon Muffins

8	**bacon slices**	8	
2 cups	**flour**	500 mL	
2 Tbsp	**sugar**	30 mL	
1 Tbsp	**baking powder**	15 mL	
½ tsp	**salt**	2 mL	
1½ cups	**cheddar cheese**, shredded	375 mL	
1	**egg**, beaten	1	
1 cup	**milk**	250 mL	
3 Tbsp	**butter**, melted	45 mL	

Makes 12 muffins.

Preheat oven to 400°F.

Cook bacon & crumble.

Into a large bowl, sift the dry ingredients. Add cheese & bacon. Make a well.

In a separate bowl combine the egg, milk & melted butter. Mix well & pour into the dry ingredients. Stir batter only until moist.

Pour into greased muffin tins. Bake at 400°F. for 20 minutes or until nicely browned.

Laura Hawthorn's Banana Pecan Muffins

3 large	**ripe bananas**	3 large	
¾ cup	**brown sugar**	180 mL	
1	**egg**	1	
⅓ cup	**cooking oil**	85 mL	
1½ cups	**flour**	375 mL	
1 tsp	**baking soda**	5 mL	
1 tsp	**baking powder**	5 mL	
½ tsp	**salt**	2 mL	
2 Tbsp	**wheatgerm** or **bran**	30 mL	
½ cup	**pecans** or **walnuts**, chopped	125 mL	

Makes 12-16 large muffins.

Preheat oven to 350°F.

Mash bananas & put into a large bowl. Add sugar & egg & beat until smooth. Stir in the oil.

Sift flour, baking soda, baking powder & salt, stir in wheatgerm or bran & add to the banana mixture. Stir only until ingredients are blended. Gently mix in ¼ cup (60 mL) of the nuts.

Spoon batter into 12-16 large muffin cups & sprinkle remaining ¼ cup (60 mL) nuts on top.

Bake at 350°F. for 15-20 minutes.

The people at Dunbar United Church in Vancouver have a "Muffin Brunch" on the second Sunday in September each year to get the church school and other activities off and running. "It's great fun," says Joan Prentice. "And everybody loves these muffins."

Joan Prentice's **Rhubarb Muffins**

1¼ cups	**brown sugar**	310 mL
½ cup	**oil**	125 mL
1	**egg**	1
2 tsp	**vanilla**	10 mL
1 cup	**buttermilk** or **sour milk**	250 mL
1½ cups	**rhubarb**, diced	375 mL
2½ cups	**flour**	625 mL
½ tsp	**salt**	2 mL
1 tsp	**baking soda**	5 mL
1 tsp	**baking powder**	5 mL
TOPPING:		
⅓ cup	**sugar**	85 mL
1 Tbsp	**butter**, melted	15 mL
1½ tsp	**cinnamon**	7 mL

Makes 16 muffins.

Preheat oven to 400°F.

Combine brown sugar, oil, egg & vanilla in large bowl & mix well. Add the buttermilk & rhubarb & stir well.

Sift flour, salt, soda & baking powder together. Add all at once to liquid mixture. Mix until just blended & fill muffin cups.

Combine the sugar, butter & cinnamon & sprinkle over muffins—press gently into batter.

Bake at 400°F. for 15-20 minutes or until tops spring back.

The topping tends to make rather messy eating for "little people". The cinnamon can be added to the batter with the dry ingredients & topping deleted—they taste just as good.

Rub-a-dub-dub...
Here's a grace the Rev. Gail Christy once used for a Sunday School dinner:

> "Rub-a-dub dub,
> Thanks for the grub.
> Yeah God!"

Muffins are always popular at church bake sales. Especially this recipe that comes from Anne Mueller of Sicamous, B.C. It's moist, fine textured, and freezes well.

Anne Mueller's
Pumpkin Muffins

2 cups	brown sugar	500 mL
1½ cups	oil	375 mL
4	eggs	4
2½ cups	flour	625 mL
2 tsp	baking powder	10 mL
2 tsp	baking soda	10 mL
½ tsp	salt	2 mL
2 tsp	cinnamon	10 mL
2 cups	pumpkin, canned	500 mL
1½ cups	raisins	375 mL

Makes 3 dozen.

Preheat oven to 350°F.

Combine sugar & oil & mix well. Add eggs, one at a time, mixing well after each addition.

Sift flour, baking powder, soda, salt & cinnamon together & add to oil mixture. Stir in pumpkin & raisins. Do not overmix. Fill muffin tins ⅔ full.

Bake at 350°F. for 20 minutes.

This recipe can also be baked as 2-9" x 5" (22.5 x 12.5 cm) loaves. Bake at 350°F. for 1 hour.

Home-cooked pumpkin may be used. Bake, rather than steam, the pumpkin to keep it from becoming watery, otherwise more flour may be needed.

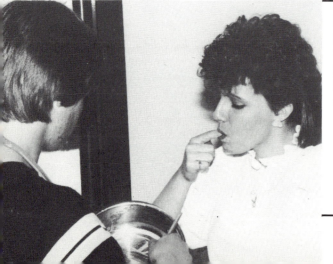

Jesus told them still another parable: "The Kingdom of heaven is like this. A woman takes some yeast and mixes it with a bushel of flour until the whole batch of dough rises."

Matthew 13: 33

It's always nice to be able to make something that is both tasty and good for you. Gwen Finlayson of Kelowna, B.C. sent this recipe for muffins that have a tasty oatmeal base. The blueberry option is also a big hit.

Gwen Finlayson's
Carrot-Oat Muffins

1 cup	**rolled oats**	250 mL
1 cup	**buttermilk**	250 mL
1 cup	**flour**	250 mL
1 tsp	**baking powder**	5 mL
½ tsp	**baking soda**	2 mL
1 tsp	**salt**	5 mL
1	**egg**	1
1 tsp	**vanilla**	5 mL
1 cup	**carrots**, grated	250 mL
⅓ cup	**oil**	85 mL
⅔ cup	**brown sugar**	170 mL
¼ cup	**raisins**	60 mL
¼ cup	**peanuts**, chopped,	60 mL

Makes 1 dozen.

Preheat oven to 400°F.

Combine oats & buttermilk in a small bowl; let stand.

Combine flour, baking powder, baking soda & salt; set aside.

Beat egg together with vanilla, grated carrot, oil & brown sugar & add to buttermilk mixture. Add this combined mixture all at once to dry ingredients. Stir just until moistened. Stir in raisins & peanuts. Spoon into muffin tins, lined with papers.

Bake at 400°F. for 15-20 minutes.

Blueberry option: decrease oil to ¼ cup, (60 mL) & increase brown sugar to ¾ cup (180 mL). Substitute ¾ cup (180 mL) fresh or frozen blueberries in place of carrots, raisins & peanuts & follow same method with remaining ingredients.

A sense of humor...
We've all heard of fowl suppers, but in St. John's, Newfoundland, they had a *Church Mouse Lunch*. That's how it was advertised!

Actually, Marjorie George of Corner Brook, Newfoundland, says the St. John the Evangelist Anglican Church Women have a sense of humor and know how to get people's attention. The lunch was soup, crackers, and cheese.

Here's something that's really popular. This recipe came at us from all directions; from Esther Faubert of Sicamous (B.C.) United Church, the U.C.W. of Palermo United Church in Oakville, Ontario, Barbara Ferris of Kelowna, B.C., and Lily Granigan of the Rosedale United in Wainwright, Alberta.

If you make it once, you'll see why it's a favorite. You can keep the batter on hand in the refrigerator for fresh-from-the-oven muffins in less time than it takes to tell about it.

And our editors have given us a bonus. There's a honey butter recipe that is just marvelous, served with warm muffins.

Everybody's Refrigerator Bran Muffins

1 cup	**shortening** or **vegetable oil**	250 mL
2 cups	**sugar**	500 mL
4	**eggs**	4
5 cups	**flour**	1.25 L
3 cups	**all-bran**	750 mL
2 cups	**bran flakes**	500 mL
1-2 cups	**raisins** or **dates,** chopped	250-500 mL
1 cup	**nuts,** chopped	250 mL
5 cups	**buttermilk**	1.25 L
5 tsp	**baking soda**	25 mL

Makes 6-8 dozen.

In a very large bowl, cream the shortening & sugar together. Add the eggs one at a time beating well after each addition.

Combine flour, all-bran, bran flakes, dates & nuts. Stir the baking soda into the buttermilk. Add the dry ingredients & buttermilk alternately to the creamed mixture.

Keep batter in tightly covered container in refrigerator & bake as needed at 400°F. for 20 minutes. Batter may be kept up to 6 weeks.

Honey Butter

1 cup	**honey**	250 mL
1 cup	**butter**	250 mL
1	**egg yolk**	1

Combine all ingredients and beat at least 8 minutes until fluffy. Keep in refrigerator.

Hazel Backus of Vancouver sent this "relative" of the carrot cake. It's interesting, unusual, and made with "on hand" ingredients. A similar recipe using beets and carrots came from Margaret Schneider of Meadow Lake, Sask.

Another pleasant not-too-sweet bread comes from Marg Young who is active in the Presbyterian Church in Vancouver.

Marg Young's Irish Soda Bread

3 cups	**flour**	750 mL
1 Tbsp	**baking powder**	15 mL
1 tsp	**baking soda**	5 mL
1 tsp	**salt**	5 mL
¼ cup	**sugar** or **honey**	60 mL
1½ cups	**currants** or **raisins**	375 mL
2	**eggs**, beaten	2
1¾ cups	**buttermilk**	430 mL
2 Tbsp	**oil**	30 mL

Makes 2 small loaves.

Preheat oven to 350°F.

Sift together flour, baking powder, baking soda, salt & sugar in mixing bowl; stir in currants.

Combine eggs, buttermilk & oil in a small bowl. Make a well in dry ingredients & pour in buttermilk mixture. Mix well with wooden spoon.

Grease & flour 2 small loaf pans. Divide batter evenly between.

Bake at 350°F. for 45-50 minutes. Test for doneness with toothpick.

Hazel Backus' Pineapple Carrot Loaf

2	**eggs**	2
½ cup	**oil**	125 mL
1 cup	**sugar**	250 mL
1 cup	**carrots**, grated	250 mL
4 Tbsp	**crushed pineapple**	60 mL
½ cup	**raisins, nuts** (or both)	125 mL
1 tsp	**vanilla**	5 mL
1½ cups	**flour**	375 mL
½ tsp	**salt**	2 mL
½ tsp	**baking soda**	2 mL
½ tsp	**cinnamon**	2 mL

Makes 1 large loaf.

Preheat oven to 325°F.

In a large mixing bowl, beat together eggs, oil & sugar. Add grated carrots, crushed pineapple (with a little of the juice), raisins or nuts, & vanilla.

Sift together flour, salt, baking soda & cinnamon & add to first mixture. Combine thoroughly & turn into a greased & floured loaf pan, 9" x 5" (22.5 x 12.5 cm).

Bake at 325°F. for 80 minutes, or until a toothpick inserted in center comes out dry. Cool completely before slicing.

This spicy loaf comes from Gertrude Rella of Sacred Heart Catholic Church in Rossland, B.C. It freezes well and is delicious sliced and spread with butter.

Gertrude Rella's Apple Sauce Loaf

½ cup	**butter**	125 mL
1½ cups	**brown sugar**	375 mL
2 tsp	**baking soda**	10 mL
2 cups	**apple sauce**, unsweetened	500 mL
3 cups	**flour**	750 mL
1 tsp	**baking powder**	5 mL
½ tsp	**salt**	2 mL
1 tsp	**cloves**	5 mL
1 tsp	**nutmeg**	5 mL
1 tsp	**cinnamon**	5 mL
2 cups	**raisins**	500 mL
½ cup	**walnuts**, chopped	125 mL

Makes 1 large loaf.

Preheat oven to 325°F.

Cream butter & brown sugar in large mixing bowl. Combine baking soda with apple sauce & add to creamed mixture.

Sift flour, baking powder, salt, cloves, nutmeg & cinnamon. Stir into creamed mixture, lastly adding raisins & walnuts. Combine thoroughly.

Spoon into a greased & floured loaf pan, 9″ x 5″ (22.5 x 12.5 cm).

Bake at 325°F. for 1½ hours, or until toothpick inserted in center comes out dry. Cool completely before slicing.

A grace...

> Christ lives in you and me
>   like the yeast within the bread.
> He is the food
>   by which our hungry souls are fed.
> His presence is to us
>   a power, like the yeast
>   that causes bread to rise,
>   to make an ample feast.
> As we break bread together,
>   let us feed on the bread of life.

There's a big office building in Toronto that houses the national staff of the United Church of Canada. If there's a concentration of church supper experts anywhere, it's got to be at "85 St. Clair."

Anne Squire heads the department that looks after the training and placing of clergy. "Our staff parties are our 'church suppers'," she says. "They fill the same need and serve the same great dishes."

Anne sent along a recipe for a moist cake that'll keep for days. If it lasts that long. She also sent along a favorite "grace" used at these staff parties, which we've included on the previous page.

Grace Kanwisher of Pleasant Park Baptist Church in Ottawa sent us a similar recipe.

Photo: Berkeley Studio

Anne Squire's Coffee Cake

BASE:
1 cup	**butter**	250 mL
1 cup	**sugar**	250 mL
3	**eggs**	3
1 tsp	**vanilla**	5 mL
2 cups	**flour**	500 mL
1 tsp	**baking soda**	5 mL
1 tsp	**baking powder**	5 mL
½ tsp	**salt**	2 mL
1 cup	**sour cream**	250 mL

TOPPING:
½ cup	**brown sugar**	125 mL
¼ cup	**white sugar**	60 mL
1 tsp	**cinnamon**	5 mL
1 cup	**walnuts**, chopped	250 mL

Makes 12-15 servings.

Preheat oven to 350°F.

Cream the butter, add sugar & mix well. Add the eggs, one at a time, beating 1 minute per egg. Add vanilla.

Sift together flour, baking soda, baking powder & salt. Add to egg mixture alternately with the sour cream.

Combine brown sugar, ¼ cup (60 mL) white sugar, cinnamon & walnuts.

Pour half the batter into a 9" x 13" (22.5 x 32.5 cm) greased pan; sprinkle with half the topping, add remaining batter, then remaining topping.

Bake at 350°F. for 35 minutes.

If you sometimes decide to bake a cake, then half way through you'd rather opt for muffins, here's the recipe for you. The batter works for either one. It's from Gwen Finlayson of Kelowna, B.C.

Gwen Finlayson's Cranberry Bread

1 Tbsp	**flour**	15 mL
1½ cups	**cranberries**, chopped	375 mL
½ cup	**nuts**, chopped	125 mL
½ cup	**raisins**	125 mL
2 cups	**flour**	500 mL
1½ tsp	**baking powder**	7 mL
½ tsp	**baking soda**	2 mL
½ tsp	**salt**	2 mL
1 cup	**sugar**	250 mL
¼ cup	**butter**	60 mL
1	**egg**, slightly beaten	1
¾ cup	**orange juice**	180 mL
1 Tbsp	**orange rind**	15 mL

Makes 1 large loaf.

Preheat oven to 350°F.

Sprinkle 1 Tbsp (15 mL) flour over cranberries, nuts & raisins on waxed paper; toss to coat & set aside.

Sift 2 cups (500 mL) flour, baking powder, baking soda & salt into large bowl; stir in sugar. Cut butter into flour mixture till crumbly.

Beat egg with orange juice & rind in small bowl. Stir into flour mixture until moist. Lastly, fold in cranberry-nut mixture.

Spoon into greased & floured loaf pan, 9" x 5" (22.5 x 12.5 cm).

Bake at 350°F. for 65 minutes or till toothpick inserted in center comes out clean. Cool on rack completely before cutting.

Cranberries may be fresh or frozen. For muffins, line 18 tins with paper muffin liners & bake at 375°F. for 20 minutes.

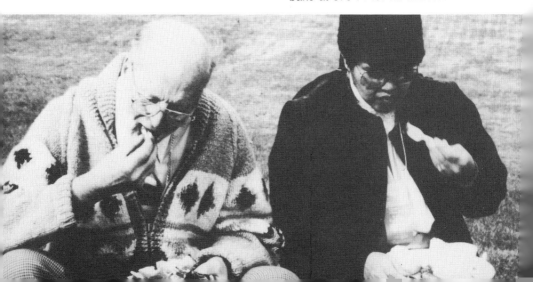

If you'd like to make an impression without making a lot of work for yourself, Diane Hoornaert of Winfield, B.C. has this suggestion. This streudel is impressive looking and easy to make. It also freezes well.

Diane Hoornaert's Simple Apple Streudel

2½ cups	**flour**	625 mL
1 tsp	**salt**	5 mL
1 cup	**shortening** or **lard**	250 mL
1	**egg yolk**	1
½ cup	**milk** (approx.)	125 mL
1 cup	**cornflakes**, crushed	250 mL
8	**apples** (preferably 'Delicious' variety)	8
¾ cup	**sugar**	180 mL
1 tsp	**cinnamon**	5 mL
1	**egg white**	1
1½ cups	**icing sugar**	375 mL
2 Tbsp	**water**	30 mL

*For easy clean-up line baking pan with tin foil.

Makes about 24 pieces.

Preheat oven to 400°F.

In large mixing bowl combine flour & salt. Cut in shortening with pastry blender (or 2 knives) till texture of fine crumbs.

Beat egg yolk in glass measuring cup; add enough milk to measure *barely* ⅔ cup (170 mL). Pour milk mixture over crumbs, working in with a fork. Finally, work with hands to form a smooth ball. Cut ball in half.

On lightly-floured surface roll half the pastry to fit a jelly roll pan, with sides, about 10" x 14"(25 cm x 35 cm). Carefully slide pastry into pan, supporting with rolling pin. This is *not* difficult, as pastry is very pliable!

Sprinkle crushed cornflakes evenly over pastry.

Peel, core & slice apples thinly. Arrange over cornflakes. Mix sugar & cinnamon together & sprinkle over sliced apples.

Roll remaining pastry to fit top. Lay over apples, cutting off excess pastry at sides. (Do not seal edges *or* cut air holes in top.)

Brush slightly beaten egg white over surface.

Bake at 400°F. for 45-50 minutes, or till golden brown.

Cool on wire rack.

Mix icing sugar & water till smooth; drizzle over streudel. Cut in serving-size pieces.

Here's a gorgeous German coffee cake from Eva Bartee, of the United Church in Westbank, B.C. She not only sent us the recipe for the cake itself, but for three different toppings.

Don't let the lengthy directions scare you. The editors have included just enough detail to ensure success for those not raised on "kuchen". By the way, baked kuchen freezes very well.

Eva Bartee's
Kuchen (Coffee Cake)

DOUGH:

1 cup	**water**, lukewarm	250 mL
1 cup	**milk**, scalded & cooled to lukewarm	250 mL
1 Tbsp	**yeast**	15 mL
1 tsp	**sugar**	5 mL
7 cups	**flour**, divided	1.75 L
6 Tbsp	**butter**	90 mL
1 cup	**sugar**	250 mL
1 tsp	**salt**	5 mL
4	**eggs**	4

Makes 3 large pans.

Combine lukewarm water & milk in warmed bowl. Dissolve the yeast & 1 tsp (5 mL) sugar in the liquids. Add 3 cups (750 mL) flour & beat until smooth. Let rise in a warm place until foamy.

Meanwhile, in a large bowl, cream the butter & gradually add sugar, creaming until light; add salt. Add 3 of the eggs, one at a time, beating well after each addition.

Stir the foamy yeast mixture & add to the butter, sugar & eggs. Gradually beat in the remaining 4 cups (1 L) flour to make a soft dough.

Turn out on floured board & knead until smooth. Some additional flour may be required but use as little as possible. Place dough in a large greased bowl, cover & set in a warm place to rise, about an hour.

When nearly doubled in bulk, punch down & turn out on a lightly-floured board. Divide dough into 3 balls. Place each on a greased cookie sheet & press out evenly with fingers, forming a thin layer with a slight rim around the edge. Brush dough with slightly beaten egg, then add the topping of your choice!

Cheese Kuchen Topping

(enough for 1 large kuchen).

10 oz	baking cheese	280 g	
1	egg	1	
¼ tsp	cinnamon	1 mL	
pinch	salt	pinch	
⅓ cup	sugar	85 mL	
⅓ cup	raisins	85 mL	
1 tsp	lemon juice	5 mL	

Combine all ingredients & spread over top of kuchen. Let rise, then bake at 325°F. for 30 minutes. Dry curd cottage cheese pressed through a sieve can be used in place of baking cheese.

Streusel Kuchen Topping

(enough for 2 large kuchen).

1 cup	flour	250 mL	
½ cup	sugar	125 mL	
¼ tsp	cinnamon	1 mL	
6 Tbsp	butter	90 mL	

Mix dry ingredients, rub in butter. Sprinkle over kuchen & let rise until doubled in bulk. Bake at 325°F. for 30 minutes.

This is a very soft streusel. For a more crumbly texture, reduce butter to 4 Tbsp (60 mL).

Apple Kuchen Topping

(makes enough for 1 large kuchen).

6-8	apples	6-8	
¼ cup	sugar	60 mL	
½ tsp	cinnamon	2 mL	

Peel & slice apples & arrange side by side to cover top of kuchen.

Mix sugar & cinnamon & sprinkle over apples. Streusel crumbs may be added, if you like, instead of sugar mixture. Allow to rise, then bake at 325°F. for 40 minutes.

An unwritten protocol...

Those marvelous church suppers sometimes had their own unwritten protocol about who brought what and how much, and who did which job. Mimi MacIntyre of the Stoney Creek United Church in Hamilton, Ontario, remembers that "there was always a big pot of beans (which my brother dreaded), and all the children carefully ate only what their family brought."

We received two brownie recipes from two well-known church leaders. Both came with interesting stories.

Walter Murray of Wolfville, N.S., sent along a recipe for "Breakfast Brownies". Walter got the recipe from Sheila Storry.

It seems the men's club at Walter's church have a breakfast get-together every Friday morning. The menu is conventional; bacon, eggs, muffins, that sort of thing. But on one occasion, there on the table was a pan of brownies.

The men knew full well the brownies didn't belong to them. But each thought of a really marvelous excuse to take just one. Or two. Walter came up with the best excuse of all—the brownie would help him write a better sermon.

That night the men repented of their sins. "Those brownies were for the Church Women's supper this evening..." was the first thing Georgina Morine said to Walter. It wasn't the last thing she said.

Bonnie Green, who is in Toronto on the national staff of the United Church working for human rights and justice, sent her recipe for 'save-the-farmland-brownies'. "In my community, saving prime farmland is a goal we've been working on for years," says Bonnie. "I belong to a group called 'APPEAL' which leads the effort. To fund our work we have an awful lot of bake sales in local shopping plazas. My contribution is always the same. Brownies. No one would pay money for anything else I make, but people say these are terrific."

The recipe we present is Bonnie's, but Sheila's variation appears below it.

Bonnie and Walter's
Save-the-Farmland Breakfast Brownies

½ cup	butter	125 mL
1 cup	brown sugar	250 mL
1 tsp	vanilla	5 mL
2	eggs	2
½ cup	cocoa	125 mL
½ cup	flour	125 mL
¼ tsp	salt	1 mL
½ cup	walnuts	125 mL

Makes 8" (20 cm) square pan.
Preheat oven to 350°F.

Cream the butter, sugar & vanilla; beat in the eggs. Blend in cocoa. Stir in flour, salt & nuts.

Bake in a greased 8" (20 cm) square pan at 350°F. for 20 minutes. Brownies will be soft & seem underdone, but that's the secret of their fudginess. When cool, frost.

Sheila Storry's variation for cake-type brownies: Her recipe uses 2-1 oz (2-28 g) squares unsweetened chocolate in place of cocoa, increases the flour to ¾ cup (180 mL) & adds ½ tsp (3 mL) baking powder with the flour. Follow the same method & bake 30 minutes.

Chocolate Frosting

¼ cup	soft butter	60 mL
¼ cup	cocoa	60 mL
1 tsp	vanilla	5 mL
2 cups	icing sugar	500 mL
3 Tbsp	milk	45 mL

Cream butter, add cocoa & vanilla. Blend in icing sugar & milk alternately.

Variation: dissolve ½ tsp instant coffee in hot milk for a mocha frosting.

I'll store this meal around my waist...
They have quite a Turkey Supper every year at Forest United Church in Forest, Ontario. At the last one, they found a poem written on one of the placemats when they were cleaning up.

According to Rev. Bill Steadman, their minister, there's a tradition of allowing people to have as much homemade pie as they can eat. This year, one woman ate five pieces. Another person ate four, and many had two or three pieces. "As a result," says Bill, "we ran out of pie before everyone was fed."

"The meal was just delicious.
I ate up every crumb.
But then I step upon my scales,
And think, 'Boy, that was dumb!'
That's 'dumb' as in dim-witted,
Not as in mute, you see.
I'll store this meal around my waist,
As a lovely memory."

Heather Tyler of the Winfield, B.C. Missionary Church, makes some of the best desserts going. Here's one of her favorites, which is similar to matrimonial cake, but with lemon filling instead of dates.

Heather Tyler's
Lemon Squares

BASE:

⅔ cup	**butter**	170 mL
1 cup	**brown sugar**	250 mL
1 cup	**flour**	250 mL
1 cup	**rolled oats**	250 mL
1 cup	**coconut**, medium unsweetened	250 mL

FILLING:

1	**lemon**, juice & rind	1
1 cup	**sugar**	250 mL
3	**eggs**, well beaten	3
2 Tbsp	**butter**	30 mL

Makes 9″ (22.5 cm) square pan.

Preheat oven to 350°F.

Combine butter, brown sugar, flour, rolled oats & coconut in large mixing bowl. Work with pastry blender until mixture is fine crumbs. Take 1½ cups (375 mL) & set aside; press remainder into square pan.

Cook lemon juice & rind, sugar, eggs & butter in top of double boiler till thickened. Spread on top of crumb mixture. Sprinkle reserved crumbs over filling. Pat down lightly.

Bake at 350°F. for 30 minutes. Allow to cool before cutting.

This is another of those "sinfully rich" recipes that probably should be reserved for special occasions. It's one of Anne Nightingale's contributions to a church supper or bake table when she's in the mood for something special.

Anne Nightingale's Sliced Almond Bars

BASE:
½ cup	**butter**	125 mL
1¼ cups	**flour**	310 mL
¼ cup	**sugar**	60 mL
1	**egg yolk**, beaten	1
½ tsp	**vanilla**	2 mL

Makes 9" (22.5 cm) square pan.

Preheat oven to 325ºF.

In a mixing bowl, cut butter into flour & sugar, as for pastry. Stir in beaten egg yolk & vanilla. Finally work into a ball with hands.

Press dough onto bottom & ½" (1 cm) up the sides of square pan. Bake at 325ºF. about 25 minutes.

TOPPING:
3 Tbsp	**butter**	45 mL
2 Tbsp	**milk**	30 mL
½ cup	**sugar**	125 mL
1 Tbsp	**honey**	15 mL
1 cup	**almonds**, sliced	250 mL

Meanwhile, in small saucepan, heat butter & milk till butter is melted. Add sugar, honey & almonds & stir well.

Spread over partially-cooked pastry. Return to oven & bake another 20-30 minutes, till golden brown.

Cool on rack 15 minutes, then cut in squares; leave in pan till completely cooled. (Freezes well.)

No one believes we could make that money...

"Church suppers make no economic sense," according to Rev. John Shearman of Palermo, Ontario. "If you balance the true cost of production against the revenue yielded, the bottom line is a deficit.

"Church suppers and teas raise good money because all the labor is free. The labor is never counted in. Neither is the cost of ingredients. A loaf of sandwiches may cost five dollars in ingredients.

"No one believes that we could have raised that kind of money just by asking for it. People have to earn it, even if church suppers make no economic sense."

Sheila Gear of Dunbar United Church in Vancouver sent this recipe. It's basically a thin shortbread base with a cream puff topping. This is a deliciously different slice, that's best served the same day.

Sheila Gear's Almond Puff

BASE:

½ cup	**butter**	125 mL
1 cup	**flour**	250 mL
3 Tbsp	**water**	45 mL

Makes 24 slices.

Preheat oven to 350°F.

In bowl, cut butter into flour. Add water. Round into ball. Divide in half. On ungreased cookie sheet roll each half to a 3" x 12" (7.5 x 30 cm) rectangle.

TOPPING:

½ cup	**butter**	125 mL
1 cup	**water**	250 mL
1 cup	**flour**	250 mL
¼ tsp	**almond extract**	1 mL
3	**eggs**	3

Bring butter & water to a rolling boil in medium saucepan. Remove from heat & quickly stir in flour & extract. Stir over low heat to form a ball. Remove from heat. Beat in 3 eggs all at once until smooth. Divide in half & spread over rectangles.

Bake at 350°F. for 1 hour until brown & crispy. Cool.

FROSTING:

¼ cup	**butter**	60 mL
1¾ cups	**icing sugar**	385 mL
¾ tsp	**vanilla**	4 mL
2 Tbsp	**cream**	30 mL
¼ cup	**almonds**, chopped	60 mL

Cream butter; stir in about ¼ cup (60 mL) of sugar gradually; stir in the vanilla. Stir in remaining sugar, adding a few drops of cream as frosting becomes thick.

Frost the Puff & sprinkle with chopped almonds before frosting dries. Cut into diagonal slices & serve.

Rev. Gail Cleaver Christy of Yellow Grass, Saskatchewan always liked the "gooey" squares at church suppers. She thought we should include one of those recipes.

This one came from Anna Coles of the West Point Grey Presbyterian Church. A similar recipe came from Marjorie and Wallace Smith of Ellerslie, P.E.I.

This sweet square is put together in the baking pan which saves washing mixing bowls.

Anna Coles' Seven Layer Squares

½ cup	**butter**	125 mL
1 cup	**graham wafer crumbs**, crushed fine	250 mL
1 cup	**coconut**, unsweetened	250 mL
¾ cup	**chocolate chips**	180 mL
¾ cup	**butterscotch chips**	180 mL
14 oz	**sweetened condensed milk**, tin	398 mL
¾ cup	**walnuts** or **pecans**, chopped	180 mL

Makes 9" (22.5 cm) square.

Preheat oven to 325°F.

Melt butter in cake pan. Sprinkle graham crumbs over this & blend, spreading crumbs in an even layer.

On top of crumb layer, spread the remaining ingredients in layers in the following order: coconut, chocolate chips, butterscotch chips, sweetened condensed milk & nuts.

Bake 30-40 minutes at 325°F. When almost cool, cut into small squares but leave in pan until completely cool.

The bread we eat is Jesus' bread...

Here's a poem by Rev. Walter Farquharson of Saltcoats, Saskatchewan. It can be used as a prayer before a meal. Or it can be sung. It has been set to music by Ron Klusmeier.*

The Bread We Eat

The bread we eat is Jesus' bread
  and it is sweet and good.
The bread we eat is Jesus' bread,
  so now we share our food.
For Jesus came to open doors,
  to help set prisoners free.
And when you've eaten Jesus' bread,
  it changes you and me.

The bread we eat is Jesus' bread
  and it is sweet and good.
The bread we eat is Jesus' bread,
  so now we share our food.
For Jesus came to show God's love,
  to name God's family.
And when we've eaten Jesus' bread,
  Our hearts begin to see.

*Music available from: The Gentle Clowns, Box 100, Cascade, Wisconsin, 53011

This is a moist "snacking" cake with a fresh orange flavor that comes from Sue Sewell of Kamloops, B.C. Sue is on the staff of Kamloops United Church as a congregational worker.

Sue Sewell's
California Cake

1 cup	**raisins**	250 mL
1	**orange**	1
⅓ cup	**walnuts**	85 mL
2 cups	**flour**	500 mL
1 tsp	**baking soda**	5 mL
1 tsp	**salt**	5 mL
1 cup	**sugar**	250 mL
½ cup	**shortening**, softened	125 mL
1 cup	**milk**, divided	250 mL
2	**eggs**, unbeaten	2

Makes a 9" x 13" (22.5 x 32.5 cm) cake.

Preheat oven to 350°F.

Rinse raisins under hot water. Cut orange into sections & grind with raisins & walnuts in blender.

Sift flour, soda, salt & sugar into large mixing bowl, add shortening & ¾ cup (180 mL) milk & beat for 2 minutes. Add eggs & ¼ cup (60 mL) milk & beat for 2 more minutes. Add orange mixture & blend.

Bake in greased pan at 350°F. for 40-50 minutes.

TOPPING:

¼ cup	**orange juice**	60 mL
¼ cup	**sugar**	60 mL
½ tsp	**cinnamon**	2 mL

Combine ingredients for topping.

When baked, remove from oven & immediately paint the topping mixture on cake top *or* ice with an orange butter icing when cool.

A dinner lubricates business.
William Scott

This large, moist, "self-frosting" cake is a great choice to take along on a camping trip. It comes from Connie Spooner of Edmonton, and was sent to us by her sister, Willa Nowell of Westbank, B.C. This cake has been to church suppers all over the west. Eye appealing and yummy!

Connie Spooner's Date Chocolate Chip Cake

1 cup	**dates**, chopped	250 mL
1¼ cups	**boiling water**	310 mL
¾ cup	**butter**	180 mL
1 cup	**sugar**	250 mL
2	**eggs**	2
2 cups	**flour**	500 mL
1 tsp	**baking soda**	5 mL
½ tsp	**salt**	2 mL
1 Tbsp	**cocoa**	15 mL

TOPPING:

½ cup	**walnuts**	125 mL
6 oz pkg	**chocolate chips**	175 g
¼ cup	**sugar**	60 mL

Makes a 9" x 13" (22.5 x 32.5 cm) cake.

Preheat oven to 350°F.

Pour boiling water over chopped dates in small bowl. Allow to cool, stir well.

Cream butter & sugar; add eggs & beat well. Sift together flour, baking soda, salt & cocoa & add to creamed mixture alternately with dates. Pour into greased pan.

Combine topping ingredients & spoon over batter.

Bake at 350°F. for 35 minutes. Test for doneness with toothpick.

Sit down and feed, and welcome to our table.
    Shakespeare

The United Church Women of Langley, B.C. undertook an interesting project recently. They held a "bake exchange", including recipes. Those were all collected into a little "goodie book". And Mrs. Linda Prouten sent us a copy for this book. The recipe our editors liked best says it all in the name. This is a dandy lunch box cake.

The Ruth Unit
Yum Yum Cake

½ cup	butter	125 mL
1 cup	sugar	250 mL
1 tsp	vanilla	5 mL
1	egg	1
2 cups	flour	500 mL
1½ tsp	baking powder	7 mL
¼ tsp	baking soda	1 mL
¼ tsp	salt	1 mL
¾ cup	buttermilk	180 mL
1 cup	marshmallows, miniature	250 mL
½ cup	chocolate chips	125 mL
TOPPING:		
2 Tbsp	butter	30 mL
¼ cup	brown sugar	60 mL
½ cup	pecans or walnuts chopped	125 mL

Makes a 9" (22.5 cm) square cake.

Preheat oven to 350°F.

In large mixing bowl, cream butter & sugar till fluffy. Add vanilla & egg & beat well.

Sift flour, baking powder, baking soda & salt. Add dry ingredients & buttermilk alternately to creamed mixture.

Stir in marshmallows & chocolate chips. Turn into greased pan.

For topping, cream the butter & brown sugar & mix in nuts. Drop small amounts of topping over cake by spoonfuls.

Bake at 325°F. for 45 minutes, or till a toothpick inserted in the center comes out clean.

> If you wish to grow thinner,
>   diminish your dinner,
> And take to light claret
>   instead of pale ale;
> Look down with an utter
>   contempt upon butter,
> And never touch bread
>   till it's toasted—or stale.
>   H.S. Leigh

This is a great cake to bake in the summertime when there's plenty of zucchini around. And it doesn't need any icing.
It comes to us from Irene Hallisey of St. Pius X Catholic Church in Kelowna.

Irene Hallisey's
Chocolate Zucchini Cake

½ cup	butter	125 mL
1 cup	brown sugar	250 mL
½ cup	white sugar	125 mL
½ cup	oil	125 mL
3	eggs	3
1 tsp	vanilla	5 mL
½ cup	buttermilk	125 mL
2½ cups	flour	625 mL
2 tsp	baking soda	10 mL
½ tsp	salt	2 mL
½ tsp	allspice	2 mL
½ tsp	cinnamon	2 mL
¼ cup	*cocoa	60 mL
3 cups	zucchini, grated	750 mL
1 cup	chocolate chips	250 mL

Makes a 9" x 13" (22.5 x 32.5 cm) cake.

Preheat oven to 325°F.

Cream butter, sugars & oil together in a large bowl. Add eggs, (beating after each), vanilla, buttermilk & mix well.

Measure flour, soda, salt, allspice, cinnamon & cocoa into a sifter & sift into the bowl. Mix well. Add well-drained grated zucchini a little at a time, mixing well after each addition to prevent the zucchini sticking together in lumps.

Pour batter into greased & floured pan. Sprinkle chocolate chips on top & bake at 325°F. for 45 minutes. Remove from pan to cool.

*If you want to cut down on the chocolate you are eating, carob powder can be substituted for cocoa without affecting taste.

The more the merrier; the fewer, the better fare.
                John Palgrave

It's always great when a delicious treat also has nutritional value. These two recipes are both from Kelowna, B.C. people; the Health Squares from Irene Hallisey of St. Pius X Catholic Church and the Whole Wheat Cake from Carol Fletcher, who is active in the Winfield United Church.

Carol Fletcher's
Whole-wheat Sponge Cake

6	large eggs separated	6
1½ cups	brown sugar	375 mL
½ cup	water	125 mL
½ tsp	vanilla	2 mL
½ tsp	lemon juice or extract	2 mL
¼ tsp	almond extract	1 mL
1½ cups	whole-wheat flour, sifted	375 mL
¼ tsp	salt	1 mL
1 tsp	cream of tartar	5 mL

Makes a 10" (25 cm) tube cake.

Preheat oven to 325°F.

Beat yolks, sugar, water & flavorings 7 minutes in a medium bowl until thick & creamy.

Sift flour & salt together twice, then add gradually to the yolk mixture.

Beat egg whites & cream of tartar until stiff. Fold into the egg yolk mixture & pour into ungreased 10" (25 cm) tube pan.

Bake at 325°F. for 60-70 minutes.

Invert & let cool thoroughly before removing from pan.

Irene Hallisey's
Health Squares

¾ cup	butter	180 mL
1 cup	brown sugar	250 mL
½ tsp	salt	2 mL
2 Tbsp	corn syrup	30 mL
2 tsp	vanilla	10 mL
2 cups	rolled oats	500 mL
¾ cup	raw wheat germ	180 mL
½ cup	sesame seeds	125 mL
½ cup	raw sunflower seeds, shelled	125 mL
½ cup	coconut, unsweetened	125 mL
½ cup	chocolate chips	125 mL

Makes 9" x 13" (22.5 x 32.5 cm) pan.

Preheat oven to 325°F. (300°F. if using heat-proof glass pan).

In a large saucepan melt butter, stir in brown sugar, salt, corn syrup & vanilla.

Add oats, wheat germ, sesame seeds, sunflower seeds & coconut & mix very well. Pack into ungreased pan & bake for 40 minutes or until a golden color. Do not overbake.

Remove from oven & immediately sprinkle with chocolate chips. As they melt, spread chocolate evenly over the top. When cool, cut into squares.

This delightful cake has been a favorite of Joan and Walter Farquharson's for many years. "We used it to celebrate most birthdays," they write. "It was a favorite for church bake sales and something our family wanted to take as dessert any time potluck suppers occurred at the church, or when they volunteered at school or in youth groups to bring a cake."

Walter and Joan live in Saltcoats, Saskatchewan, where Walter is the United Church minister. He's also known internationally as a very fine hymn writer. Several of his hymns are in the Anglican-United Hymn Book

This cake has a fine, moist texture, and a pleasant coffee flavor.

Joan and Walter's Coffee Chiffon Cake

2 Tbsp	**instant coffee**	30 mL
1 cup	**hot water**	250 mL
6	**eggs**, separated	6
¼ tsp	**cream of tartar**	1 mL
2 cups	**sugar**, divided	500 mL
1 tsp	**vanilla**	5 mL
2 cups	**flour**	500 mL
2 tsp	**baking powder**	10 mL

Makes a 10" (25 cm) tube cake.

In a small bowl, dissolve instant coffee in the hot water.

In a large bowl, beat egg whites until foamy, add cream of tartar. Gradually beat in ¾ cup (180 mL) of the sugar. Beat until stiff peaks form.

Beat egg yolks & vanilla together, add 1¼ cups (310 mL) of the sugar, beating until the sugar is dissolved.

Sift flour & baking powder together. Beat into the egg yolk mixture alternately with the coffee.

Fold the yolk mixture into the beaten egg whites. Pour into an ungreased 10" (25 cm) tube pan. Bake at 375°F. for 1 hour.

Invert & allow to cool thoroughly before removing from pan.

Mary Henderson of Calgary is a remarkable person. Among many other things, she is the Past Moderator of the Christian Church (Disciples of Christ) in Canada.

She's also a judge of fine food. This impressive-looking cake with an unusual flavor really impressed our editors. They took it to coffee hour after church, and it received rave reviews.

Mary Henderson's Poppy Seed Chiffon Cake

½ cup	poppy seeds	125 mL
1 cup	boiling water	250 mL
7	egg whites	7
½ tsp	cream of tartar	2 mL
2 cups	flour	500 mL
3 tsp	baking powder	15 mL
1½ cups	sugar	375 mL
1 tsp	salt	5 mL
½ cup	oil	125 mL
2 tsp	vanilla	10 mL
7	egg yolks	7
¼ tsp	baking soda	1 mL

Makes a 10" x 4" (25 x 10 cm) tube cake.

Pour boiling water over poppy seeds & let stand 2 hours.

Place egg whites in large glass bowl, add cream of tartar; beat until very stiff peaks form.

In separate bowl, sift flour, baking powder, sugar & salt. Stir in oil, vanilla, egg yolks, baking soda & poppy seed mixture. Beat until smooth. Gently pour egg yolk mixture over egg whites & carefully *fold* together.

Pour into ungreased tube pan. Bake on lowest rack at 325°F. for 50 minutes, then at 350°F. for 10 minutes. Invert pan to cool.

Remove from pan when cooled. May be glazed with lemon icing if desired.

There's a tradition in the Winfield, B.C., United Church that the kids love and the adults love even more. It's the "Jesus' birthday party" held by the Sunday School each year.

A highlight of the party is a huge birthday cake. The Sunday School teachers make a bunch of different flavored 9" x 13" cakes, and arrange them together in a huge rectangle. Then Fiona Warrington's icing is used to cover all the lumps and bumps and make the cake a feast for the eye, body and spirit. Fiona now lives in Fort McMurray, Alberta, but the tradition continues.

This recipe is made with granulated sugar, and is less sweet than most.

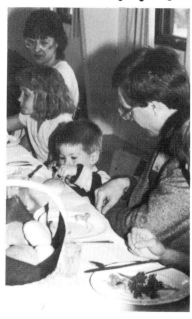

Fiona Warrington's "Jesus Cake" Frosting

¾ cup	**milk**	180 mL
3 Tbsp	**flour**	45 mL
⅔ cup	**butter**, softened	170 mL
½ cup	**granulated sugar**	125 mL
1 tsp	**vanilla**	5 mL

Makes about 2 cups (500 mL).

In a saucepan, gradually add milk to flour to make a smooth paste; cook, stirring constantly until thickened. Don't undercook! Remove from heat, cover the mixture with plastic wrap touching the surface & cool.

In bowl cream butter, sugar & vanilla until fluffy. Add cooled flour mixture by spoonfuls, beating until smooth.

Makes enough to ice an angel food cake or a large rectangle.

Tiny Tim's Toast

"God bless us everyone!"

Here's a bit of fun to have in a Bible study group sometime. Make a Scripture Cake.

This very unique recipe came from Helen Shearman of Oakville, Ontario, and Madeline Ingledew of Victoria, B.C.

The recipe works. Elaine and Anne tried it. The result is a large fruit cake which lacks the variety of fruit we put in our cakes today—cherries and pineapples are not mentioned in the Bible.

The fun with Scripture Cake is in decoding the recipe. An experienced cook should be able to make a good cake just by looking at the Scripture passages. But if you get stuck, Elaine and Anne have listed the ingredients for you in a more conventional form.

Be sure to use the King James translation of the Bible. Read a little of what goes before and after the passage indicated, just to get the flavor of what that portion of scripture is about. And have fun!

Helen and Madeline's Scripture Cake

1½ cups	Judges 5:25 (last clause)	½ cup	Judges 4:19 (last clause)
2 cups	Jeremiah 6:20 (sugar)	2 cups	I Samuel 30:12 (raisins)
2 Tbsp	I Samuel 14:25	2 cups	Nahum 3:12
6	Jeremiah 17:11	1 cup	Numbers 17:8
4½ cups	I Kings 4:22		
2 tsp	Amos 4:5 (baking powder)		
½ tsp	Leviticus 2:13		
to taste	II Chronicles 9:9		

Follow Solomon's prescription for making a good boy, Proverbs 23:14 and you will have a good cake.

Need some help? Here is the recipe as we tested it.

1½ cups	**butter**	375 mL
2 cups	**sugar**	500 mL
2 Tbsp	**honey**	30 mL
6	**eggs**	6
4½ cups	**flour**	1.12 L
2 tsp	**baking powder**	10 mL
½ tsp	**salt**	2 mL
½ tsp	**cinnamon**	2 mL
¼ tsp	**nutmeg**	1 mL
¼ tsp	**cloves**	1 mL
½ cup	**milk**	125 mL
2 cups	**raisins**	500 mL
2 cups	**figs**, chopped	500 mL
1 cup	**almonds**, blanched & slivered	250 mL

Makes 2-9" x 5" (22.5 x 33.5 cm) loaves.

Preheat oven to 300°F.

Cream butter, sugar & honey together; add eggs one at a time, beating well after each addition.

Sift flour, baking powder, salt & spices together. Add to creamed mixture alternately with milk.

Stir in fruit & nuts & spoon into 2 loaf pans which have been greased & lined with waxed paper.

Place pan of water on bottom rack of oven. Bake at 300°F. for 2½-3 hours.

If you enjoy coconut, you'll love these macaroons. They come from Joy Quigley of Kelowna B.C., and are an attractive addition to any sweet tray.

Joy Quigley's
Coconut Macaroons

2	egg whites	2
¼ tsp	salt	1 mL
1 Tbsp	cornstarch	15 mL
1 cup	sugar	250 mL
½ tsp	vanilla	2 mL
1½ cups	coconut, medium unsweetened	375 mL

Makes about 2 dozen.

Preheat oven to 350°F.

Beat egg whites in top of double boiler until stiff. Add salt, cornstarch & sugar. Continue beating until well combined (the sugar doesn't have to dissolve).

Set over boiling water & cook 5 minutes, stirring constantly. Remove from heat & add vanilla & coconut. Drop by teaspoonfuls onto a greased cookie sheet.

Bake at 350°F. for 10-12 minutes, or until set & lightly browned.

Allow to cool on cookie sheet about 2 minutes before removing to rack.

What do Ethel Buck of Ryerson United in Vancouver and Brian Jackson of Trinity United in Vernon, B.C. have in common besides their denomination?

They both enjoy Welsh Cakes. Try them, and you'll discover the delightful nutmeg flavor of these pastry-like griddle cakes. They're nice to make during hot weather, because you don't need to heat the oven to make them.

Ethel Buck's Welsh Cakes

2 cups	flour	500 mL
¾ cup	sugar	180 mL
2 tsp	baking powder	10 mL
½ tsp	salt	2 mL
1 tsp	nutmeg	5 mL
¾ cup	butter	180 mL
½ cup	currants	125 mL
2	eggs	2
1 tsp	vanilla	5 mL

Makes about 3 dozen cookies.

Sift together into a bowl flour, sugar, baking powder, salt & nutmeg. With a pastry blender cut in the butter until very fine. Add the currants & mix.

Beat eggs & vanilla & add to mixture, blending with a fork as you would in making pastry.

On floured board, roll dough to about 1/8″ (.3 cm) thickness & cut out with cookie cutter. Cook on ungreased medium hot griddle, about 4 minutes each side.

Be gentle when you touch...

>Be gentle
>>when you touch bread.
>>>Let it not lie
>>>>uncared for, unwanted.
>>>>>So often bread
>>>>>>is taken for granted.
>>>There is so much beauty
>>>>in bread—
>>Beauty of sun and soil.
>>Beauty of patient toil.
>>Winds and rains have caressed it.
>>>Christ has often blessed it.
>>Be gentle
>>>when you touch bread.

Author unknown

Here's a great idea for a kids' Christmas party. These crisp, gently spiced rolled cookies are perfect for cutting into special shapes.

They make good Christmas tree ornaments. You can cut a hole for the string in the unbaked cookie with a drinking straw.

Elaine Towgood's Gingerbread Cookies

½ cup	**butter**	125 mL
½ cup	**shortening**	125 mL
1 cup	**sugar**	250 mL
½ cup	**brown sugar**	125 mL
1	**egg**	1
¼ cup	**light molasses**	60 mL
3½ cups	**flour**	875 mL
2 tsp	**baking soda**	10 mL
2 tsp	**cinnamon**	10 mL
1 tsp	**ginger**	5 mL
½ tsp	**cloves**	2 mL

Makes 8 dozen cookies.

Cream butter, shortening & sugars together, add egg & molasses & cream thoroughly.

Sift together flour, soda & spices; stir into creamed mixture & chill well.

Preheat oven to 375°F.

On lightly floured surface, roll dough to ¼" (.5 cm). Cut with cookie cutter & place 1" (2.5 cm) apart on ungreased cookie sheet; sprinkle lightly with sugar for sparkle.

Bake at 375°F for 7-8 minutes. Remove to rack & cool.

Confectioner's Icing
(for decorating cookies).

| 2 cups | **icing sugar** | 500 mL |
| 2 Tbsp | **light cream**, about | 30 mL |

Add enough light cream to icing sugar to make the consistency of a stiffly beaten egg. This frosting is easy to work using an icing tube.

I have noticed that when chickens quit quarreling over their food, they often find that there is enough for all of them. I wonder if it might not be the same way with the human race.

Don Marquis

Ilene Patterson of Winfield, B.C., has many memories that connect food and church.

Ilene walked into town with her family each Sunday morning for church at 11:00 and stayed through lunch because Sunday School was at 2:00 and there wasn't enough time to walk home in between.

"I remember mother's canned chicken in sandwiches of homemade bread. For dessert, we had Trillbies. They were my Dad's favorite."

Ilene is the editor of *The High-way*, the newspaper of the Anglican Diocese of Kootenay. She tells us that in the dictionary, the word "trill" means to "roll or turn over".

A similar recipe came from Hazel Baldwin of Westbank, B.C.

Ilene Patterson's Trillbies (Oatmeal Cookies)

1 cup	**sugar**	250 mL
3 cups	**oatmeal**	750 mL
2½ cups	**flour**	625 mL
1 tsp	**salt**	5 mL
1 tsp	**baking soda**	5 mL
1 cup	**shortening**	250 mL
1 cup	**buttermilk**	250 mL

Makes 7-8 dozen.

Preheat oven to 375°F.

In a large mixing bowl, combine dry ingredients thoroughly & cut in shortening as for pastry. Pour buttermilk over oatmeal mixture, stirring in thoroughly. Continue stirring until buttermilk is absorbed & finally work with hands to form a ball.

Working with about ¼ of the "ball" at a time, roll to about 1/8" (.3 cm) thickness, flouring board & rolling pin when necessary. Cut into circles with cookie cutter & place on cookie sheets (can be put close together).

Bake at 375°F for 8-10 minutes.

When cool, store in covered tin.

*These would also be good sandwiched together with a date filling!

FILLING:

1 lb	**dates**	450 g
¼ cup	**sugar**	60 mL
1 cup	**boiling water**	250 mL

Combine ingredients & simmer over medium heat till thick, stirring occasionally. Cool. Sandwich baked cookies together with filling.

When you mention church suppers, Sr. Katherine McCaffrey, RSCJ, of Ottawa immediately remembers the lobster or salmon suppers in Atlantic Canada. "It was delicious food, often served outdoors in an atmosphere of friendliness and joy."

Sr. Katherine has another memory that points to the real importance of church suppers. "As a child, long before the ecumenical movement, my most pleasant and positive memories of Christians of other faiths came from attending their church suppers."

That experience may have been a preparation for the work she's doing now. Sr. Katherine is the Assistant General Secretary of the Canadian Religious Conference.

However, there is a problem with the recipe for gingersnaps which she sent. It's almost impossible to eat just one. And they're equally good fresh from the oven or days later.

A similar recipe called "Newfie Cookies" was contributed by Dorothy Scott of Westbank, B.C.

Sr. Katherine's Gingersnaps

1 cup	shortening	250 mL
1 cup	sugar	250 mL
1 cup	molasses	250 mL
1	egg	1
2¾ cups	flour	680 mL
1 Tbsp	ginger	15 mL
1 Tbsp	baking soda	15 mL
½ tsp	salt	2 mL
¼ tsp	allspice	1 mL

Makes about 6 dozen.

Cream shortening & sugar till fluffy; add molasses & egg, beating well.

Sift together flour, ginger, baking soda, salt & allspice. Stir into creamed mixture, combining thoroughly. Chill mixture in fridge several hours.

Preheat oven to 350°F.

Grease baking sheets. Drop cookie mixture by spoonfuls & flatten with fork (or the bottom of a glass), dipped in sugar.

Bake at 350°F. about 12 minutes, or till lightly browned. Remove to rack to cool. Store in covered tin.

"The only thing I don't like about church suppers is that they don't happen often enough," says Karen Holmes. Karen is studying for the ministry at the Vancouver School of Theology, and prior to that, had the rather unique experience of being the "Youth Moderator" of the United Church of Canada for two years.

Karen probably can't afford to make these cookies. It's not that they're expensive. It's just that you couldn't make a batch big enough to satisfy the students (or the faculty for that matter) at V.S.T.

In fact, our editors recommend you double the recipe for this very crisp cookie. Otherwise, you'll just have to make another batch tomorrow.

Karen Holmes' Oatmeal Chocolate Chip Cookies

½ cup	butter	125 mL
½ cup	sugar	125 mL
½ cup	brown sugar	125 mL
1	egg, beaten	1
1 Tbsp	water	15 mL
½ tsp	vanilla	2 mL
¾ cup	flour	180 mL
½ tsp	baking soda	2 mL
½ tsp	salt	2 mL
1½ cups	rolled oats	375 mL
1 cup	chocolate chips	250 mL

Makes 4 dozen.

Preheat oven to 375°F.

Cream butter, add the sugars, then the egg, water & vanilla.

Sift flour, soda & salt together. Add to creamed mixture.

Add rolled oats & chocolate chips & mix well.

Drop by teaspoonfuls onto greased cookie sheet & bake at 375°F. for 10 minutes or until light brown.

Results benefiting everybody...
Majorie Smith, who is the organist at the Conway United Church, and her husband Wallace, who is an elder, remember the "fellowship and caring; the working together to achieve results benefiting everyone" that characterized church suppers in Ellerslie, P.E.I. Wallace sends this cheerful poem:

> "The more you give, the more you get.
> The more you laugh, the less you fret.
> The more you do unselfishly,
> The more you live abundantly."

Here's a rich dough that's easier to work with than pastry. It comes from Ivy Fallow of the Winfield United Church.

Any not-too-sweet jam or jelly makes a good filling.

Ivy Fallow's
Apricot Tarts

1½ cups	flour	375 mL
3 Tbsp	sugar	45 mL
2 tsp	baking powder	10 mL
pinch	salt	pinch
½ cup	butter	125 mL
1	egg, beaten	1
3 Tbsp	milk	45 mL
1 cup	apricot jam	250 mL

Makes 20-2" (5 cm) tarts.

Preheat oven to 375°F.

Sift flour, sugar, baking powder & salt into a bowl. Add the butter & cut in with a pastry blender.

Combine beaten egg & milk. Stir into flour mixture with a fork. Add more milk if dough does not stick together easily.

On floured surface, roll out dough as you would for pastry. Cut into 3" (7.5 cm) squares. Fit squares into tart pans. Place about 1 tsp (5 mL) of jam in the center of each. Bring the 4 corners of the dough to the center & squeeze together.

Bake at 375°F. for 15-20 minutes or until golden brown.

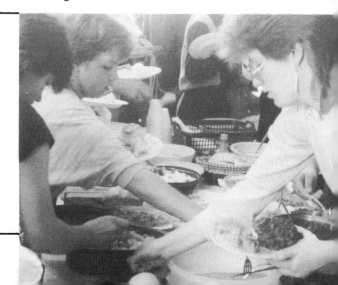

Ever thought of having a church supper in a barn? That's what they do in Orangeville, Ontario.

"Our United Church Women's group began serving Strawberry Suppers in the barn twenty years ago," says Betty Fines. "Our small, country church is over one hundred years old, and still standing is the horse shed that held the horses and carriages while people worshipped.

"Every June the shed is opened, aired and cleaned for the Annual Strawberry Supper. Some of the six or seven hundred people that come to the Strawberry Supper come for the smorgasbord salad dinner, but most of them come for those strawberries and delicious homemade butter tarts."

It's probably at that event that Betty earned her "degree" of B.T.M. (Best Tart Maker). And if she ever put her butter tarts out on a bake table, they wouldn't last a minute before being sold.

In testing this recipe, Elaine and Anne decided to cut back on the sugar a bit. Betty's recipe called for 3¾ cups of brown sugar. You can make your own decisions about that.

Betty Fines' Butter Tarts

PASTRY FOR TARTS:

2½ cups	**flour**	625 mL	Makes 4 dozen small tarts.
2 Tbsp	**sugar**	30 mL	Mix together flour, sugar & salt. Cut in shortening & butter till fine crumbs.
½ tsp	**salt**	2 mL	
½ cup	**shortening**	125 mL	Combine egg & water, toss with fork to make soft dough. Shape into ball with hands & *gently* knead about 5 times on lightly floured surface.
¼ cup	**butter**	60 mL	
1	**egg**, beaten	1	
2 Tbsp	**cold water**	30 mL	

Cut ball in half & work with half at a time. Roll out to about 1/8" (.3 cm) thickness; cut with 3" (7.5 cm) round cookie cutter & line small tart tins.

Preheat oven to 350°F.

FILLING:

4	**eggs**	4	Beat eggs in mixing bowl. Add sugar, butter, vanilla, *choice* of raisins, currants, coconut or nuts & nutmeg, if desired. Stir well.
2 cups	**brown sugar**	500 mL	
3 Tbsp	**butter**, melted	45 mL	
1 tsp	**vanilla**	5 mL	
½ cup	**raisins, currants, coconut** or **nuts**	125 mL	Spoon filling into unbaked tart shells, taking care not to overfill.
¼ tsp	**nutmeg** (optional)	1 mL	

Place on bottom rack of preheated 350°F. oven & bake for 20 minutes.

Christian stories always end with a beginning; with a resurrection. This cookbook is no exception. It ends with a recipe that not only makes a good cake, it makes a good sermon illustration. Or at least a good story for the children.

There's a tradition at the United Church in Armstrong, B.C., around the refreshments served every Sunday after church. "There are always a few goodies left over. These are carefully saved and frozen. About once a month, we have saved enough for our 'cake'.

"Every cake is different," says Majorie Glaicar, the Social Convenor at Zion United, "because we never start with the same mix of leftovers. Cakes, cookies, tarts, muffins, scones or whatever may be used."

This recipe is easily doubled or tripled.

Zion United's Resurrection Cake

9" square	**pastry**	22.5 cm
3 Tbsp	**jam**, any flavor	45 mL
¼ cup	**shortening**	60 mL
½ cup	**sugar**	125 mL
1	**egg**	1
1 tsp	**vanilla**	5 mL
2 tsp	**baking powder**	10 mL
1 tsp	**cinnamon**	5 mL
4 cups	**cake crumbs**, etc., approx.	1 L
1 cup	**milk**	250 mL

Makes 9" (22.5 cm) square cake.

Preheat oven to 350°F.

Grease cake pan, then line with pastry. Spread jam over bottom.

Cream shortening & sugar, add egg & vanilla.

Into 2 cups (500 mL) of crumbs, mix baking powder & cinnamon. Add crumbs, baking powder & spice to the creamed mixture alternately with milk. Add remaining 2 cups (500 mL) of crumbs or as many as necessary to make a thick pour batter. Pour over jam & pastry.

Bake at 350°F. for 30-40 minutes. When cool, frost with a butter icing—maple flavored is nice.

Index

Almond Bars	161	
Almond Puff	162	
Alsatian Baeckoffe	88	
Antipasto, Trinity	24	
Appetizers	**23-28**	
Apple Kuchen Topping	157	
Apple Sauce Loaf	152	
Apple Streudel, Simple	155	
Apple Torte, Bavarian	111	
Apricot Tarts	179	
Baked Beans	106	
Baked Brunch Souffle	104	
Baking	**137-181**	
Banana Pecan Muffins	146	
Bannock	144	
Barbecued Chicken Wings	94	
Bavarian Apple Torte	111	
Beans, Baked	106	
Beans, Hula Hula	106	
Beef Main Dishes	**78-89**	
Beef, Braised in Barbecue Sauce	89	
Beet Salad, Molded	58	
Beverages	**15-22**	
Biscuits, Bannock	144	
Biscuits, Drop	145	
Blueberry Muffins	149	
BOP	18	
Borsch, Chilled	40	
Braised Beef/with Barbecue Sauce	89	
Bran Muffins, Refrigerator	150	
Bread, Irish Soda	151	
Broccoli Cheese Squares	60	
Broccoli Cream Soup	38	
Brownies, Save-the-Farmland Breakfast	159	
Buns, German	139	
Buns, Instant Yeast	140	
Burgers, Tuna	71	
Butter Tarts	180	
Charlotte Joynt's Marshmallow Squares	124	
Cabbage Rolls	82	
Cabbage Salad, Genevieve's	50	
Cabbage Salad, Pickled	51	
Cake, California	164	
Cake, Chocolate Zucchini	167	
Cake, Coffee	153	
Cake, Coffee Chiffon	169	
Cake, Coffee Kuchen	156	
Cake, Date Chocolate Chip	165	
Cake, Poppy Seed Chiffon	170	
Cake, Resurrection	181	
Cake, Scripture	172	
Cake, Whole Wheat Sponge	168	
Cake, Yum Yum	166	
California Cake	164	
Calypso Punch	21	
Carrot-Oat Muffins	149	
Carrot Salad, Gujerati	47	
Carrot Salad, Marinated	48	
Casserole, Chicken	97	
Casserole, Chili Con Carne	80	
Casserole, Hot Rice	66	
Casserole, Johnny Mazetti	79	
Casserole, Kalamalka	63	
Casserole, Macaroni and Cheese with Tomato	102	
Casserole, Scallop	72	
Casserole, Sea Shell	76	
Casserole, Shipwreck	78	
Casserole, Tomato	63	
Casserole, Vegetable	61	
Casserole, West Coast Shrimp or Crab	74	
Casserole, Wild Rice	67	
Casserole, Zucchini-Tomato	62	
Cauliflower Soup	36	
Cheddar Bacon Muffins	146	
Cheese Crisps	23	
Cheese Kuchen Topping	157	
Cheese Souffle	103	
Cheese & Spinach Squares	59	
Cheese Squares, Broccoli	60	
Cheese Straws	23	
Cheesecake, Mom's	116	
Cheesecake, No-Bake	113	
Cheesecake, Pistachio Almond	115	
Cheesecakes	**111-116**	
Chicken, Barbecued	94	
Chicken Casserole	97	
Chicken Cordon Bleu	95	
Chicken Main Dishes	**90-97**	
Chicken Paprikas	96	
Chicken, Crispy Fried	94	
Chicken, Curried	93	
Chicken, Koinonia	92	
Chicken, Noella's	91	
Chicken, Orange-Onion	90	
Chiffon Cake, Poppy Seed	170	
Chiffon Cake, Coffee	169	
Chili Con Carne	80	
Chilled Oyama Borsch	40	
Chilled Soup, Gazpacho	39	
Chilled Soup, Pluma Moos	41	
Chocolate Chip Oatmeal Cookies	178	
Chocolate Frosting	159	
Chocolate Upside-Down Pudding	132	
Chocolate Zucchini Cake	167	
Chowder, Clam	35	
Chowder, Fish	34	
Chowders and Soups	**31-41**	
Cioppino	32	
Clam Chowder	35	
Coconut Macaroons	173	
Coffee Cake	153	
Coffee Cake, Kuchen	156	
Coffee Chiffon Cake	169	
Coffee Fantasia	22	
Coleslaw, Pickled	51	
Confectioner's Icing	175	
Cookies, Coconut Macaroon	173	
Cookies, Gingerbread	175	
Cookies, Gingersnaps	177	
Cookies, Oatmeal	176	
Cookies, Oatmeal Chocolate Chip	178	
Cookies, Trillbies	176	
Cookies, Welsh Cakes	174	
Cordon Bleu, Chicken	95	
Cottage Cheese Salad, Lemon	57	
Cream of Broccoli Soup	38	
Crab Casserole, West Coast	74	
Crab Mousse	26	
Cranberry Bread	154	
Cranberry Refrigerator Dessert	117	
Crepes, Easy	134	
Crisps, Cheese	23	
Crispy Fried Chicken	94	
Date Chocolate Chip Cake	165	

Index — 183

Desserts	111-134	
Devilled Egg Casserole	100	
Dip, Eggplant	28	
Dip, Shrimp	27	
Dips	27,28	
Doughnuts, Spudnuts	141	
Dressing, Italian Cheese	46	
Dressing, Tomato	46	
Drinks	15-22	
Drop Biscuits	145	
Dumplings, Chicken Paprikas	96	
Easy Crepes	134	
Eggplant Dip	28	
Eggs, Hot Devilled	100	
Eggs, Scotch	101	
Fancy Sandwich Loaf	107	
Fantasia, Coffee	22	
Filling, Mocha Mousse	134	
Fish Chowder, Maritime	34	
Fish Steaks with Sour Cream Sauce	77	
Flora's Dessert	114	
Fresh Peach Pie	130	
Frosting, Chocolate	159	
Frosting, Confectioner's	175	
Frosting, "Jesus Cake"	171	
Fruit Salad, Haroset	120	
Fruit Soup	41	
Gazpacho	39	
Genevieve's Salad	50	
German Buns	139	
German Potato Salad	65	
Gingerbread Cookies	175	
Gingersnaps	177	
Gujerati Carrot Salad	47	
Hamburger Casserole, Johnny Mazetti	79	
Hamburger Casserole, Shipwreck	78	
Hamburger Casseroles	78-87	
Hamburger Soup	33	
Haroset	120	
Hashed Brown Potato Casserole	64	
Health Squares	168	
Honey Butter	150	
Hors d'oeuvres	23-28	
Hot Devilled Eggs	100	
Hot Rice Salad	66	
Hula Hula Beans	106	
Instant Breakfast, BOP	18	
Instant Yeast Buns	140	
Irish Soda Bread	151	
Italian Cheese Dressing	46	
Italian Meatball Stew	86	
Japanese Salad, Sunomono	49	
Jellied Salad, Vegetable	58	
"Jesus Cake" Frosting	171	
Johnny Mazetti	79	
Jungle Juice	22	
Kalamalka Casserole	63	
Koinonia Chicken with Rice	92	
Kuchen (Coffee Cake)	156	
Kuchen Topping, Apple	157	
Kuchen Topping, Cheese	157	
Kuchen Topping, Streusel	157	
Lasagne, Wolfville	84	
Layered Lettuce Salad	52	
Lemon Cottage Cheese Salad	57	
Lemon Delight	123	
Lemon Pie	127	
Lemon Squares	160	
Lemonade Syrup	15	
Lettuce Salad, Layered	52	
Liberation Pancakes	108	
Linguine, Tomato Cheese	83	
Loaf, Apple Sauce	152	
Loaf, Cranberry Bread	154	
Loaf, Pineapple Carrot	151	
Macaroni Shrimp Salad	55	
Macaroni and Cheese with Tomato	102	
Macaroons, Coconut	173	
Main Dishes	71-108	
Marinated Carrot Salad	48	
Maritime Fish Chowder	34	
Marshmallow Refrigerator Salad	56	
Marshmallow Squares, Charlotte Joynt's	124	
Meatball Stew, Italian	86	
Meatballs, Presbyterian Spaghetti and	85	
Meatless Main Dishes (Almost)	100-108	
Men's Club Meatloaf	87	
Meringue, Pavlova	131	
Millionaire Dessert	119	
Mintel, Raspberry	20	
Mocha Mousse Filling	134	
Molded Beet Salad	58	
Mom's Cheesecake	116	
Motorcycle Rolls	137	
Mousse, Crab	26	
Muffins, Banana Pecan	146	
Muffins, Blueberry	149	
Muffins, Carrot-Oat	149	
Muffins, Cheddar Bacon	146	
Muffins, Pumpkin	148
Muffins, Refrigerator Bran	150
Muffins, Rhubarb	147
No-Bake Cheesecake	113
Noella's Chicken Dish	91
Oatmeal Chocolate Chip Cookies	170
Orange-Onion Chicken	90
Pancakes	108
Paprikas, Chicken	96
Party Potato Salad	54
Passover Curried Chicken	93
Pasta Dishes	83-85
Pastry for Tarts	180
Pastry, Almond Puff	162
Pavlova	131
Peach Mallow Pie	122
Peach Pie	130
Pickled Coleslaw	51
Pie, Fresh Peach	130
Pie, Lemon	127
Pie, Peach Mallow	122
Pie, Pumpkin	126
Pie, Raisin	129
Pie, Rhubarb Custard	128
Pies	126-130
Pineapple Carrot Loaf	151
Pineapple Pork Chops	99
Pistachio Almond Cheesecake	115
Pluma Moos	41
Poppy Seed Chiffon Cake	170
Pork Adobo	98
Pork, Pineapple	99
Potato Salad, German	65
Potato Salad, Party	54
Potatoes, Hashed Browns	64
Potatoes, St. Luke	64
Presbyterian Spaghetti and Meatballs	85
Pudding, Chocolate Upside-Down	132
Pumpkin Muffins	148
Pumpkin Pie	126
Punch, Calypso	21
Punch, Rhubarb	16
Punch, Strawberry	17
Quadraphonic Delight	112
Quiche, Salmon Crunch	73
Quiche, Surprise Pie	75
Raisin Pie	129
Rapid Rolls	138
Raspberry Mintel	20
Refrigerator Bran Muffins	150

Refrigerator Dessert, Cranberry	117	Soup, Cauliflower	36	Worth Remembering Tuna Burgers	71
Resurrection Cake	181	Soup, Cream of Broccoli	38	Yeast Buns, Instant	140
Rhubarb Custard Pie	128	Soup, Hamburger	33	Yeast Rolls, Motorcycle	137
Rhubarb Muffins	147	Soup, Veal Sour	31	Yeast Rolls, Rapid	138
Rhubarb Punch	16	Spaghetti, Presbyterian	85	Yeast Rolls, Talami	142
Rhubarb Sponge	121	Spanikopeta	105	Yum Yum Cake	166
Rolls, German Buns	139	Spinach Pie	105	Zucchini, Chocolate Cake	167
Rolls, Instant Yeast	140	Spinach Salad	53	Zucchini-Tomato Casserole	62
Rolls, Rapid	138	Spinach Squares, Cheese	59		
Rolls, Talami	142	Sponge Cake, Whole Wheat	168		
Rolls, Motorcycle (Orange)	137	Spudnuts	141		
Salad, Genevieve's Cabbage	50	Squares, Health	168		
Salad, German Potato	65	Squares, Lemon	160		
Salad, Gujerati Carrot	47	Squares, Seven Layer	163		
Salad, Hot Rice	66	Squares, Sliced Almond	161		
Salad, Japanese	49	St. Luke Potatoes	64		
Salad, Jellied Vegetable	58	Stew, Alsatian Baeckoffe	88		
Salad, Layered Lettuce	52	Stew, Italian Meatball	86		
Salad, Lemon Cottage Cheese	57	Strawberry Angel Torte	118		
Salad, Macaroni Shrimp	55	Strawberry Punch	17		
Salad, Marinated Carrot	48	Strawberry Slice	125		
Salad, Molded Beet	58	Straws, Cheese	23		
Salad, Party Potato	54	Streudel, Simple Apple	155		
Salad Seasoning	45	Streusel, Kuchen Topping	157		
Salad, Spinach	53	Sunomono	49		
Salad, Sunomono	49	Surprise Pie	75		
Salad, Twenty-Four Hour	56	Syrup, Lemonade	15		
Salads	**45-58**	Talami	142		
Salads and Veggies	**45-67**	Tarts, Apricot	179		
Salmon Crunch Quiche	73	Tarts, Butter	180		
Salmon or Trout Steaks	77	Tomato Casserole	63		
Sandwich Loaf	107	Tomato Cheese Linguine	83		
Scallop Casserole	72	Tomato Dressing	46		
Scotch Eggs	101	Tomato-Zucchini Casserole	62		
Scottish Trifle	133	Torte, Bavarian Apple	111		
Scripture Cake	172	Torte, Strawberry Angel	118		
Sea Shells	76	Trifle, Scottish	133		
Seafood	**71-77**	Trillbies (Oatmeal Cookies)	176		
Seasoning for Salad	45	Trinity Antipasto	24		
Seven Layer Squares	163	Tuna Burgers	71		
Save-the-Farmland Breakfast Brownies	159	Twenty-Four Hour Salad	56		
Shipwreck Casserole	78	Upside-Down Pudding, Chocolate	132		
Shrimp Casserole, West Coast	74	Veal Sour Soup	31		
Shrimp Dip	27	Vegetable Casserole	61		
Shrimp Salad, Macaroni	55	Vegetable Jellied Salad	58		
Simple Apple Streudel	155	**Veggies**	**59-67**		
Sliced Almond Bars	161	West Coast Shrimp or Crab Casserole	74		
Soda Bread, Irish	151	Welsh Cakes	174		
Souffle, Baked Brunch	104	Whole Wheat Sponge Cake	168		
Souffle, Cheese	103	Wild Rice Casserole	67		
		Wolfville Lasagne	84		